Tales

From the Wrong Side of the Couch

A Psychiatrist Looks Back on His Work

Drew Bridges

 iUniverse®

TALES FROM THE WRONG SIDE OF THE COUCH
A PSYCHIATRIST LOOKS BACK ON HIS WORK

Each story in this book represents something I experienced. Nothing is made up in its entirety. However, in order to protect the identity of patients, teachers, and peers, I have taken care to change demographics, names and other features of the stories.

iUniverse books may be ordered through booksellers or by contacting:

iUniverse
1663 Liberty Drive
Bloomington, IN 47403
www.iuniverse.com
844-349-9409

ISBN: 978-1-6632-5076-6 (sc)
ISBN: 978-1-6632-5077-3 (e)

Library of Congress Control Number: 2023902513

Print information available on the last page.

iUniverse rev. date: 02/20/2023

Contents

Acknowledgements

Many thanks to my writing group: Gale, Christy, Bill, Lauren, and Robin for their thoughtful criticism at every stage of the writing process.

Introduction

This is a book of stories. These "tales" shine light on the irony and complexity of life. That makes them stories worth telling, worth hearing, or reading. The events described in this book happen to be about my becoming and working as a psychiatrist.

Of course, bewildering experiences of life are not limited to the world of medicine and mental health. Despite the specialized setting from which I offer them, I intend these stories for a broad audience of readers. I think there is a universality to what is told here.

The stories in this work are not strictly organized along theme or timeline, since this is not an autobiography or even a traditional memoir. I do follow a general structure of starting with early years of my training then moving to later years of working in the profession. I started medical school in 1971 and practiced psychiatry for 40 years, until retirement in 2015.

I did not set out to write this book as any sort of expose or call for reform of the profession. I intended to avoid polemics and let the stories speak for themselves. However, during the writing of it I concluded there are some judgements about the house of medicine that beg to be delivered.

Still, overall, there is no villain or "bad guy" unless that would be my own embarrassing cluelessness at that time of my life about how the world works, within the profession and beyond. I would like to think I learned a great deal and grew in knowledge and perspective over time, but I'm sure a measurable portion of my cluelessness persists.

Above all, I have worked to be respectful to my patients. In the instances that I needed to talk about the people coming for mental health evaluation and treatment, I have changed demographic and situational details that might identify them. Only broad categories of psychiatric disorders are described in any depth.

I have also tried to be respectful, kind, and "forgiving" to my teachers and fellow students. However, some in each category, professor and peer alike, demonstrated their own awkward limitations in understanding the world in which they worked and otherwise traveled. No actual names are used, with one exception. In one story it was necessary to give some first names to make a point about gender-neutral names.

One note about the title: I am not trained as a psychoanalyst, so I did not make use of the analyst's couch in my practice. However, the couch is the definitive, iconic symbol of the profession, or at least it was when I was in training. I could not resist using it in the title as a "hook" for the stories. If this offends some, I apologize. Controversy might be a good thing by drawing some attention to the book and helping me sell more copies. Selling books is one of the goals of this writing; I'm not above shameless self-promotion for the purpose of commerce.

The Sorcerer's Apprentice

First Day as a Psychiatrist: July 1975

With medical school completed, and the University of North Carolina in Chapel Hill granting me admission to the psychiatric specialty program, I came eagerly to day one of three years of training necessary to become a psychiatrist. As one of a class of twelve new psychiatric students in training—eleven men and one woman, all white—I joined the others in Conference Room B, the site of most of our didactic classes and case conferences. We were now officially "resident" physicians, the term given to doctors in their years after medical school, continuing in their specialty training.

Sparsely furnished, the room was comfortable enough. We sat in heavy, straight-backed wooden chairs with solid armrests. We gathered around a large polished-wood conference table. A solitary earth-toned portrait of Sigmund Freud looked down on us from otherwise bare, neutral-colored walls.

Our new resident orientation schedule began with practicalities: where to go to get a parking pass for the university campus, a warning about a spot at one training site run by local police as a speed trap for newbies, where to collect our mail, and where to pick up paychecks. A paycheck! After paying for four years of medical school education, we were now actually getting paid. Most of us had loans to repay. The details of where our salaries came from to actually pay us a modest salary did not concern me, but some of my classmates grumbled about our status as "cheap labor" for the hospital system.

Beyond the practical matters, the first sobering item of orientation business came with instructions from a senior administrative staff member about how to fill out involuntary commitment forms. These papers empowered us to hospitalize someone against his or her will. All of us had done psychiatric rotations during medical school and knew such a thing existed, but our familiarity with the process was spotty at best. Comfort with the process was even further away. More urgently, one of us would be on-call in the hospital emergency department that night, so that lucky doctor in training needed to be ready to perform and to document this type of exam. We were assured that for our first time on call each of us would be paired with a more senior resident, so we relaxed somewhat.

Next item of business came from a senior faculty member who was there to talk with us about "personal and professional boundaries." He was a much older man, and I was later to learn, internationally well-known in the subspecialty of forensic psychiatry.

"Most of you will not need this talk, maybe none of you," he began in a grave and authoritative voice, "but every year or so, one of you, somebody in the class, gets in trouble with personal boundaries." He paused for dramatic effect and then continued with descriptions of how naïve young doctors in training had in prior years transgressed the boundaries of appropriate involvement with patients.

"Hopefully, we have screened out from the applicants anyone who is a true psychopath, but all of you are vulnerable to making a mistake, due to what you are getting yourself into in the next three years. You will see things, hear about things, and feel things in your work that will be new and sometimes overwhelming, to you." His serious demeanor, in addition to the topic in question, compelled our attention.

The professor gave two examples, by way of contrasting what kind of things could be forgiven and what would not. His first example featured a male psychiatric resident who "fell head-over-heels in love with his patient." This novice psychiatrist had unwisely chosen to blurt out his tearful, desperate love for her in a psychotherapy session and was both surprised and emotionally crushed when she ran from the building. Fortunately for both of them, he did not touch her, and he went immediately to his supervisor to ask for guidance. He was assigned his own therapist. His patient would have been given a new therapist, but she did not return the phone calls from the clinic director. This arrangement led to forgiveness for the young doctor, followed by understanding, and he continued successfully in the program.

"Most, if not all of you, are going to fall in love, or experience some other equally problematic emotion, toward your patients. Get ready. It's not real life. It's work; and it's part of the nature of the work. But you won't know that when it's happening. And the consequences are real if you don't handle it well. You'll understand more about this as the year progresses. Use your supervisor for anything about which you feel uncomfortable or think you should be uncomfortable with." I remember reflecting on how his voice conveyed both a calm, reassuring concern and, at the same time, a warning.

The second example he gave us concerned another young man who had incorporated regular breast "exams" for his female patient into the psychotherapy sessions. When he ultimately revealed this "assessment technique" to his supervisor, seemingly unaware of the inappropriateness of such behavior, he was dismissed from the program, and barred from the medical profession.

The professor ended by repeating the acknowledgement that our particular group of new residents may not need to be reminded of these kinds of "boundary violations." I wondered if he was indirectly praising us for our collective maturity and sophistication. But he did finish his talk with one final comment, "But I don't want there to be any misunderstanding...if you stick it in, we'll cut it off."

His point was well made, vivid. But I do wonder what our one female colleague thought about it.

One final agenda item for the orientation session: The Chairman of the Department of Psychiatry walked in with two senior residents, one being the Chief Resident, the class leader. These two students had asked permission to speak with the new class, and the Department Chairman was there to respond to their presentation.

I remember thinking how clean-cut the two senior residents looked. This was the '70s; my class had a good representation of long-haired guys, scruffy beards, and one who wore bell-bottomed jeans and a bold colorful shirt to our first day as psychiatrists. I had on my best corduroy pants and a short sleeved knitted shirt. But these two guys sported creased dress-pants, white shirts, and conservative ties under dark blue blazers.

The Chief Resident began, "Tonight, the second and the third-year class are going out on strike. We want you with us."

"*Strike?*" We had been psychiatrists for less than a half-day, and we're now asked to go on strike? The justification for the strike had to do with a merger between two training sites. One was the main location of the psychiatry program in Chapel Hill, at what was then called North Carolina Memorial Hospital. The second site was the state hospital in Raleigh, called Dorothea Dix Hospital. The heart of the matter, as explained by the two residents, was that this merger had developed after the previous classes had been enrolled and had begun their training. They felt truly misled about their training program.

4

The Chief Resident continued his pitch, "I don't know how many of you knew about the state hospital rotation when you signed up here, but it was news to us. A real 'bait and switch' in my opinion. What have you heard? What can I tell you about this?" He surveyed the room for our reaction. No one spoke. Blank faces all around.

He seemed frustrated that no questions came. "You are not safe at the state hospital. You will not believe what is waiting for you there. You're going to find a place that's out of control and nobody to teach you what you are up against." He shot a quick glance at the Department Chairman, who sat calmly, betraying no emotion.

Clearly deflated, if not irritated with our lack of response, the two left the room, on the way out giving us information about how to contact them with our decision. I'm not sure if anyone from my class responded to them later.

The Department Chairman spoke next. He began slowly, even sadly, about the concerns of the two senior residents. He did not talk for long, but simply told us that he would see to the quality of our experience and our safety and asked us to not "get all wrapped up in the politics of the department at this point in your training." He welcomed us to the profession and told us we were on the doorstep of a "truly remarkable and rewarding way to earn a living." Then without inviting questions, he left.

We looked around at each other and I think we all concluded the same thing. We were ready for this larger experience. Perhaps more importantly, we did know about the state hospital rotation when we were recruited. And for many of us, we were not about to mess up our first paycheck. I was actually excited about going to Dorothea Dix Hospital, named for the legendary reformer of the way of caring for the mentally ill. Having read the basic story of her life and accomplishments, I felt a kinship. At that time of my life, I was a card-carrying idealist and reformer.

I happened to be one of four residents who were to begin our rotations at the Dorothea Dix location, and I felt ready for it. I had read about current day conditions at state hospitals and the evils of institutionalization. Dorothea and I still had work to do. Something like freeing the masses from their chains.

The conflict back in Conference Room B made me even more excited about getting my start at the state hospital. My motivation was some version of going there to do something about obvious wrongs. I walked out of North Carolina Memorial Hospital and headed to Dorothea Dix, my idealism as yet unchallenged, even with what had already happened that first day. As I drove, I reflected on the power to deprive a person of freedom, warnings about castration, and what might happen with the strike.

First Night on Call at the State Hospital

My first days at Dorothea Dix were exciting and at times overwhelming. I saw human beings more disturbed than I expected. Some were unbelievably violent. Fortunately, my individual supervision from a senior staff psychiatrist was timely and helpful. I never missed an opportunity to get input from her. As the weeks rolled by, structured lectures from teaching faculty helped, as did the case conferences led by experienced psychiatrists at the state hospital.

Every so often we would rotate through the admissions area, mostly at night, where patients would be evaluated for admission. Some were voluntary; most came in police cars with as many as three or four people at a time on involuntary commitment papers. Some were from the county where Dix Hospital was situated, but others came from some distance away within the larger "catchment area" of this hospital. A total of four state mental hospitals, each with their own designated coverage area, served North Carolina.

One of my eye-opening, idealism-challenging experiences happened on my first night in admissions. A thirtyish year-old man presented himself voluntarily for admission. "I can't shake this depression. I can't stop thinking about killing myself. I got to get some help," he said.

Wearing dirty jeans, a well-worn work shirt, and an ancient and tattered leather jacket, he looked defeated and stressed, but was otherwise organized in thought and speech. His hands and the visible areas of his neck featured multiple tattoos, some artistically rendered, others clearly homemade. His shaved head and lack of eyebrows gave him a primitive or "unformed" look. I took him into one of the private exam rooms to get more information.

Five minutes into my interview with him, the staff psychiatrist in charge that night came unannounced into the room. She addressed him in a firm, no-nonsense manner. "We told you not to come back here. You will not be admitted. You need to leave."

I was confused. But the man was not surprised. "God, you again," he muttered. He pulled his jacket tightly around him and walked out the door. We followed him through the waiting room as he left. My supervisor explained it simply: this was a local drug dealer who hid out in the state hospital when one of his drug dealings went bad. Usually this involved him using the drugs himself, or supplying several girlfriends, rather than sticking to the business plan. People were looking for him to get their money.

At about that moment, his four-volume chart arrived from medical records. My supervisor, a physically "sturdy" woman ten years or so my senior, told me to take a look at the record for educational purposes. She chuckled as she explained that the man who had just been told to leave was on the "Ten Most Unwanted" list. "It's not a real list, I mean not written down," she continued, "but you'll learn soon the people who abuse the system. Should be clear from the chart how you make the list."

We were interrupted by someone yelling just outside the door.

"There's a guy out here trying to hang himself!"

We rushed through the door. Just outside, we found that the drug dealer had placed a thin rope over a brace of the metal awning and tied it around his neck. He was making a gurgling sound as he pulled the weight of his body down on the rope. I looked to my supervisor for what to do, but she had run back into the building. I moved toward the man but before I could take any meaningful action, she came bursting back outside with a pair of scissors in her hand. She went directly to him and with one motion cut the rope.

He fell to the ground. Without hesitation she took him by his upper arm and pulled him to a standing position. "Where's your truck? Where'd you park?" I jumped in and took his other arm. Within a dozen steps toward the parking lot, early enough in the evening for it to still be light outside, she recognized his "Cowboy Cadillac," so designated by his vanity front license plate. We positioned him in the front seat, identified that he was clearly not harmed by his actions, and she told him firmly once again to leave and not come back. We turned back to the building and walked away.

"Hey doc?" He called out to us from the front seat of his truck through the open window. "Remember that Dilantin prescription you wrote for me a few months ago? I got it right here." With that, he held up a pill bottle and proceeded to take one handful after another of what we later estimated were about one hundred Dilantin 300mg capsules. He rolled up his window and locked the door before we could get to him. We watched him wash down two full handfuls of pills with beer from a Papst Blue Ribbon can, as he laughed at us through closed window.

The man won. By then two security guards for the hospital had arrived. After a fifteen-minute negotiation, he complained that he was getting ready to pass out and opened the door. Security escorted and half carried him back inside where he was granted admission to the medical unit. There he received a stomach evacuation and enjoyed three-hots-and-a-cot for a couple of days. Time enough for him to make a longer-term plan to escape his creditors.

I'll bookend the situation with the man in the truck with another that happened in the last month of the rotation. In October, several cars pulled up to the door and let out close to a dozen men. They filed peacefully into the waiting room. A man who was obviously their leader explained, "We're here from the fair."

"The what?" I puzzled.

"The State Fair, we just got set up."

I was bewildered. I couldn't grasp who they were and why they were there.

"We're here to get some medicine. And couple of these guys might need a detox."

Okay. I was starting to understand. Maybe. To my credit, I did not follow my instinct to tell them to leave. I called for help from the older staff psychiatrist who was supervising me that night. He burst into the waiting room with a smile and a hug for the man who leading the group. "Heyyyy! I been lookin' for you guys! So, who's back?"

Long story short: these were some of the people, at that time in history, who put up the tents, ran the games, and did the heavy lifting of whatever at the state fair, and they had mental health needs. Many were on the road with the games and rides much of the year. The state mental hospital in Raleigh represented their only option for refills of prescriptions and alcohol detoxification services. Almost everyone in the room had been there before. All, except for one young man who needed alcohol detox, had charts on file with the hospital.

It was a busy night. We wrote a lot of prescriptions for antipsychotics, antidepressants, and Antabuse. We admitted two people for detox. That was 1975. In my eventual forty years of practice, I'm not sure I helped a more grateful, and deserving, group of patients.

Most experiences for those four months at the state hospital were not so dramatic, but ultimately the four of us figured out that the Dix psychiatrists were not "second-rate" professionals, as the Chief Resident who spoke with us on that first day would have had us believe. Perhaps, on paper, our teachers at Dix did not have the credentials of the faculty back in Chapel Hill. Most had spent their entire careers in the state hospital system rather than in the academic center. But collectively there was real wisdom within this group of professionals.

From behind one-way mirrors, we spent fascinating hours watching the leaders there interact with very sick people. Some of the psychiatrists had been there before the advent of modern drugs. They gave us the perspective that even though these medications were far from perfect, that by any measure they represented progress. More strikingly, for a small but significant fraction of the patient population, these medications deserved the term "miracle drugs." In many cases, the treatment returned patients successfully back home to family and community, some after years of hospitalization.

Another source of wisdom came from the paraprofessional staff, the "orderlies." Many of them had structured their work lives around Dorothea Dix when it was commonly called a "therapeutic community" with its own farm and indeed its own culture. Progress in medications and "human rights reforms" had wiped away that world, and on balance that was a good thing, but I came to believe that this institution was never an evil place. For many patients it was an "asylum" in the very positive sense of the word.

Slow Down, How Did I Get Here?

Getting Admitted to Medical School

It might be helpful here to describe how I arrived at the point where the profession of psychiatry generally, and the medical center of The University of North Carolina specifically, was willing to admit me to the kingdom of "shrinks." It was unlikely that this would be where I ended up. My family had no legacy of medical professionals. Even within my extended family there were few who went on to education beyond high school. Basketball scholarships got me into college and a high military draft lottery number allowed me to stay there. My college major was English literature, thanks to my experiences with the bookmobile that came to my rural childhood home.

By the time I was a senior in college I had pretty much reached my maximum level of mediocrity on the basketball court. I left the sports world after my junior year to fully embrace and wallow in all night philosophical/literary/bull sessions with some strange counter-culture people destined to become poets and writers of other sorts. (One of the group became a Wall Street guy, but that's another story).

Now lacking a basketball scholarship, I needed a way to pay for college and signed up for a job working as an orderly in a local county hospital. That was my introduction to the world of medicine. More details about that later.

Upon graduation with honors in English Literature from Lenoir Rhyne College and admitted to The University of Tennessee as a doctoral candidate, I slowly came to the realization that I had no confidence in my ability to earn a living as an English major. Gradually I had fallen in love with everything that went on in the hospital. I saw people recover from grave injuries, and some who did not survive. Through every extreme I was impressed with the skill and dedication of the medical staff, from doctors to nurses to the people who delivered patients their food and cleaned up the messes made in the process of caring for the sick.

I was especially drawn to the twelve-bed psychiatric ward on the fourth floor. There I saw people who reminded me of characters in some of my favorite works of fiction: Sartre, Steinbeck, Baldwin. The emergency room presented its own unique world, from the long hours where nothing much happened to the times when the staff exploded into action to care for people in desperate situations. I helped the Assistant Director of Nursing, a woman recently out of the military, deliver a baby in a taxi-cab right outside the ER door. I'll tell that story in detail later.

So, I told The University of Tennessee I wasn't coming for the graduate degree in English Literature and signed up for two more years of undergraduate work in the sciences at Lenoir Rhyne College. No more late-night poetry and Herman Hesse intellectual love fests. Off to the lab. Now what's the difference between a Florence flask and an Erlenmeyer? I decided to aim for medical school but settle for anything that would earn me a living in the field of medicine. The great American novel would come later in my spare time.

My grades were okay in the science courses, and when the time came to apply to medical school, I received some good advice and I got lucky. One of my college chemistry teachers told me to apply early, explaining that medical schools like to fill up a solid fraction of their class early and would be more discriminating of its applicants later on. My application was in the mail the day before the medical schools were accepting them.

The good luck came with the type of student the UNC School of Medicine was looking for in the current class. The way I understood it, there is a kind of pendulum swing that happens within admission committees. Some years they are looking for "humanists" and other years for scientists. Some classes are filled with students who already have graduate degrees in science fields, and some who had published research papers in first line medical journals. But this happened to be the year they would admit forty percent of the class with majors in other than science. My class was blessed with historians, musicians, liberal arts majors, and other non-science majors. Good for me. My medical college admission test scored me in the lower quarter in math and science but in the ninety-ninth percentile in language arts and general information.

In addition, there was a push that year to admit students from rural areas who might return home as family doctors. I marched right into my interviews and said I wanted to return home to Burke County, NC and be a general practitioner. In truth, I never seriously considered anything other than psychiatry. Incidentally, the first two interviews were with one doctor named Payne (pain) and the other named Sorrow. Some kind of sign?

An early admission letter came just weeks after my interview. More about those early years of medical school later—there are stories to tell during that time—but I think to tell it sequentially might not be as interesting as presenting it in sub-groupings with similar themes.

The next section is about the early experiences of a doctor in training. It should come as no surprise that there is a lot of sorrow and pain (Payne) in stepping into the role of a physician. Most of this is about what is experienced by the patients, but doctors and other medical professionals suffer in their own way. Medical students soon learn that it takes a little getting used to.

Preparing for the Pain and Sorrow

In the above story about the man who took the pills at the Dorothea Dix admissions unit, the reader gets a hint about the way people harm themselves, driven by emotional motivations and situations. Add to this the illnesses that seem to come out of nowhere, or from passive neglect of good health habits. Both categories are some of the key features of being a doctor. It's actually more than pain and sorrow. The word "carnage" is not wrong.

Early in my career as a psychiatrist I kept a diary of sorts describing the violent acts that my patients performed on themselves or others. This way of "working through" things that horrified me must have helped, since I stopped the diary before too long. I don't know where that document is now. Perhaps this list became a burden, or perhaps I just could not keep up with the sheer number of such acts. Or maybe I got numbed to that kind of thing, or maybe reached a level of acceptance of the world in which such things present. There is always a risk of becoming insensitive to that kind of pain, sorrow, and carnage. In the pages that follow I'll write about some of this. The reader can be the judge about whether I ended up with acceptance or insensitivity.

One form of preparation for this task came that first year in medical school, from professors of the Department of Pathology. Pathology is a general term used to describe deviation from the norm or from what is considered normal health. But it is also a medical specialty and several of the pathologists who lectured us were kind of "rock stars," genuine storytellers about how things go wrong, sometimes through no one's fault. Sometimes this came unintended from things doctors did trying to help. The pathologists were the final recipients of the remains of human carnage, performing autopsies, and often passing judgement about why it happened.

An early piece of wisdom presented to first year medical students, from one of the pathologists, went something like this: *"If you are in a hospital and think you might be getting ready to die, drag yourself to the bathroom, lock and barricade the door. Because if the doctors there figure out you are getting ready to die they will jump on you, stick needles into your muscles and blood vessels, stick tubes into every opening your body offers, make some new openings, then sometimes jump up and down on your chest, and pump you full of fluids and drugs using any path they can use, and on occasion cut you open with knives."* We laughed but understood as he told stories of the aggressive "heroics" that were performed on patients who died anyway.

As a medical student I sat in a meeting room to observe what was called a "death conference." I don't recall how the cases were chosen for review of patients who had died in the hospital. Perhaps they reviewed all hospital deaths, but the ones who were discussed at length generated heated discussions about what went wrong. Sometimes the criticism was brutal, about mistakes that were made. Mostly it was simply "earnest" with talented surgeons, pathologists, and other medical specialties trying to do the right thing.

More relevant to the specialty of psychiatry, one pathologist gave an hour-long lecture complete with graphic slides, presenting all the various ways that people intentionally killed themselves. One "case"—it's easier to talk about cases than "people"—stood out from the various guns, knives, overdoses, drownings, and suffocations. It involved a man who had taken a hammer and driven a ball-point pen into his brain. The pathologist added the following information: "And yes, it was a Bic," referring to that era's advertising about the ruggedness of that brand of ballpoint pen.

Another jarring brush with the reality of death came in the form of a tray of human organs, brought into one of our learning labs by a pathologist. This came early in my first year of medical school. These were the remains of a football player at UNC who had died of a heat stroke during a practice session. There was something about the way the doctor pulled back the cloth covering of the tray and said flatly, "This is..." and then said the player's name. He did not say these are the "remains of" the player or "this is the autopsy of." My ears heard him say this is what the person is now.

I betrayed no emotion to the others there, but in truth, I almost ran from the room, shocked, by...what? The clinical nature of dealing with death? I look back now at the number of such events that followed, in people dead and people alive but sick or injured and wonder at my sensitivity. You get used to it. If you didn't, you could not be a doctor.

I saw many examples of how these experiences turned future doctors cold, hard, and insensitive on even the most basic level. This seemed to be the acceptable alternative to being vulnerable or overwhelmed. The worst came on a neurology rotation in my third year of medical school. By way of context, the neurology ward housed some of the sickest, close-to-death patients that one would find in the hospital in 1973. They had been transferred out of intensive care because there was no treatment available that would improve or restore them. They remained in the hospital because they were too sick to go home or to any version of nursing homes available at that time.

The team that conducted rounds on this ward was comprised of a senior resident physician, a junior resident, an intern, two or three medical students, and often a nursing student or two. We would start outside the door of each patient or pair of patients, reviewing the latest clinical data.

The senior resident on that team was an energetic, charismatic, funny, and brilliant guy. He often quoted works of literature along with medical facts and he had a way of questioning the members of his team that generated fascinating and useful discussions.

We entered one room that housed two elderly men, both suffering from the ravages of alcoholism and demonstrating a common metabolic abnormality, that of a chronic and dangerously low blood sodium. The sum total of everything that was wrong with the men put both of them in comatose states. After we gathered around the beds looking to the senior resident to guide the discussion, he flashed a wicked grin and reached into the pocket of his long white coat. He pulled out a bottle of Wild Irish Rose and addressed the two unconscious men, "Okay guys, here's your last chance…first one to get his sodium up to 130 gets this bottle." He paused, cupped his hand behind his ear and continued, "I can't hear you…no takers I guess…well, that's about all I have to offer."

After we all laughed or smiled politely, a brief but characteristically dismissive discussion concluded our review of the condition and bleak future of the two men. This was one of many times I felt uncomfortable about the behavior of my superiors but said nothing. I joined the group rushing on to the next room of patients.

By far the most unsettling of these "educational" incidents came in my third year of medical school, on a pediatric rotation on the wards of the teaching hospital. As the most junior member of a team of doctors in training, most of my time was spent observing the work of the intern and others, and running necessary errands for the rest of the team.

The intern I followed on this rotation was a young woman, all business and as capable as anyone from whom I learned the early lessons of being a doctor. I accompanied her often to the pediatric intensive care unit, where one patient took an extraordinary amount of her time and energy.

The patient was an eight-year-old girl who had been comatose from tuberculosis meningitis for several months, "alive" only through artificial means, with little evidence of brain function. In the several weeks I observed the events of her care, the discussion evolved from guarded hope to the first discussions of when it would be time to accept her death and discontinue use of support machines.

Ultimately, it was the patient's parents who tearfully moved the discussion to when it was time to say goodbye. The process unfolded with discussions less about life signs and treatment options and more about being certain there was little else to be done. I saw the first hugs to the parents from the intern that led to actual discussions about when it was time to let go. To say I was impressed with the kindness and professionalism of the intern, never showing tears but always available to grieving parents, doesn't adequately describe what I observed and felt.

I also observed, with real puzzlement, that the actual task of removing the child from the life support apparatus was left to the intern. The Attending Physician, overall head of the team, did not participate in that process, nor did any of the other more senior members of the team. I watched from the back of the room as the intern, assisted by a handful of staff nurses, accompanied and administered to the young girl in the last moments of her life.

I would like to think that there were other meetings and other discussions that gave support and guidance to this young woman intern who carried out the physical steps that allowed a child to pass through the final stage of an unavoidable death. I was not present for any such meetings and my fear is that there were none. Perhaps it was simply understood that such things were part of the education of a doctor, and that the more senior members of the team had experienced their own version of this, and now it was time for the next in line to go through it.

I suppose it was not my place to question any of this. Perhaps it was my shortcoming that I could not speak up at the time, even to ask questions in the service of my education. It felt like only a heartbeat of time before we all moved on to attend to others in need.

Experiences that Challenge One's World View

Still in my third year of medical school, and twenty-seven years old, I considered myself generally "wise" about the world. I opposed the war in Vietnam, was already informed about the damage by humans to the environment, and the dangers of an overpopulated planet. I considered myself pretty-well liberated from my paternalistic impulses regarding the way women should be treated. This included supporting a woman's right to choose to terminate a pregnancy. Then came an experience that showed me I was less than a finished product in what I believed.

During my Obstetrics and Gynecology rotation, I joined a team of residents and medical students who stood outside the ward where abortions were performed.

"I need a volunteer," said the senior resident. "Gonna teach everybody how we do this."

The two other third year students simultaneously turned to look at me. "Drew's your guy," they indicated. Still not sure if this was some endorsement of me or avoidance of the task by the others.

"Okay, you're the one. Ever seen a saline abortion?" I answered no, and the resident continued. "It's pretty simple. Put a needle through the belly into the uterus, push in some salty water, and wait. Tissue remains will be extruded...in few hours. Let's go inside and I'll walk you through it. Good to go?"

My state of mind felt disturbingly close to when I once went sky diving. Not sure I really wanted to do this, but like the sky-diving instructor, the senior resident seemed confident that he knew what he was doing. Third year medical students are small players in a big world, so why not?

We entered the room as a group to encounter a teenage girl-woman accompanied by an older woman. My assumption was this was her mother, maybe a grandmother, but no one introduced anyone to anyone else. The older woman was asked politely to wait outside. A nurse held the hand of the frightened teen, and we got down to business.

"Okay, sweetheart. You ready?" the resident addressed the patient. Her eyes were glassy, but she said yes in a clear voice, then closed her eyes. She did not look up or speak throughout the procedure. A tray of medical instruments was maneuvered into place and the resident and I both put on sterile gloves. Taking our places on opposite sides of her bed, the resident gave me instructions about how to proceed. The other medical students and a junior resident stood at the back of the room.

"So, here's the needle, saline all ready to go in the syringe. Now we find the landmarks." Guided by my instructor, I placed my hands on her abdomen and felt the enlarged uterus. I remember thinking it was about the size of a small cantaloupe.

"So, you want to put the needle in right there...first we clean off the skin real good...grab those sterile pads..." My teacher talked me through it step by step, how hard to push the needle, how to pull back on the syringe to make sure you hit amniotic fluid and not a blood vessel, and then how quickly to inject the fluid that would induce contractions and lead to evacuation of the contents of the uterus. My part was over in minutes.

The resident stepped back, crossed his arms across his chest and spoke to the room. "Great job, Drew. I think you got a future with this. You okay, sweetheart?" The patient murmured a soft "un-huh."

We all rushed from the room as the older woman was told to come back in. I think I overheard the nurse giving them some information about what to expect in the next several hours. In the hallway, the resident turned and spoke to me, "So, since she's now your patient, I want you to stay behind and see how this goes. For your education… just hang around and watch. Not much that can go wrong. We'll finish the rounds. Catch up with us, check in with me when it's over."

I don't really remember how long the process took. I do recall the awkwardness of going back to the room and not knowing how to relate to either the older or the younger woman. They asked me no questions and started no conversations otherwise. I asked questions about pain and discomfort and received minimal, guarded replies. I came and went from the room, busying myself with looking at some medical papers when out of the room, and trying to appear helpful and concerned when I was in the room. A nurse seemed to be giving some comfort to the young patient, but she didn't seem to know what to do with me, so she generally ignored me.

When the process came to completion…when the "contents were extruded from the uterus," I stood in a corner of the room and watched the nurses do their job. I don't know what I expected to see, but the "contents" that were "extruded" looked a lot like a fully formed infant albeit a very small one. I remember being shocked and slightly nauseated. When I rejoined the group, things were getting busy and there was no "checking in" about what I had experienced.

22

Then it was time to move on to the next educational clinical experience, so I filed the experience away and continued to be the good student. But this became one of several truly compelling memories of my 44 years from admission to medical school to retirement from practice as a psychiatrist. I revisit it from time to time, usually when hearing political discussions about the right to choose, the intrusion of government into medical processes, the meaning of a fetal heartbeat, whether the fetus has a "soul," the appropriate stage of pregnancy when abortion is legal, and so on.

What did I learn? What do I think, or now believe about abortion, as a psychiatrist and as a person? Let me pair that experience with another and I will try to answer.

A few years later, during my psychiatric residency years, I sat in a small conference room with a clinical social worker some years my senior in age and in professional experience. Before us sat a family, all members female, including a mother, two twenty-something daughters, and the "identified patient", another 18 years old daughter. An older woman, the grandmother of the patient, completed the list of those present.

The patient was described as failing in all aspects of her life. No high school diploma, no job, a series of abusive boyfriends, one pregnancy and abortion, and ultimately a psychiatric inpatient admission for a suicidal "gesture." We were now two weeks after discharge from the hospital and meeting in the outpatient clinic to try to help her get her life on track. I should note here that the department of psychiatry had a strong "family therapy" component. A prevailing point of view, led by some of the more popular teachers in the department, was that psychiatry was trying to do too much with medicines and individual therapy. The real help should come from a "family systems" approach. I felt drawn to this concept.

After the requisite introductions and small talk around how everyone was feeling, the social worker and I gave a general introduction of what we would try to accomplish for the patient and her family. No questions came in response, but the grandmother did make a statement of enthusiasm for working with us to get something done for her young-adult grandchild.

I then stepped in with the first of a series of untimely questions. "Will her father be joining us at some point?" I received only blank stares, interrupted by information from the social worker that the father was not in touch with or involved with the daughter or her family. I would later learn that this was a family devoid of men. No personal involvement, no financial support, and no expectation that this would change. A better description of this family's legacy would be that they had all been "terrorized" in various ways by the men in their lives.

I tried to move the session on and asked, "How far are we along with (the patient) having a plan to move out into a place of her own?" In response to this question, one of the older daughters stood up and angrily blurted out a challenge. "I really don't see what we're doing here. This is nonsense." She then walked out. The patient turned her body away from me, rested her head on the back of the couch, and did not look at me again for the entire session.

The social worker tried to rescue the session, or rather, rescue me, by directing the conversation back to gathering general information about the family. This succeeded to a limited extent, but the hour ended with a request from the grandmother. "We also were wondering if maybe there was a medicine that would make her not feel so bad about herself."

So, back to the question of what did I learn from these experiences? I learned how little I knew about the larger world, for instance, that abortion is more than a supreme court argument. I learned that my middle class 1950s-1960s television sit-coms version of families needed revision. My narrow set of life experiences was on full display, and I was humbled.

What do I now think about abortion? One of my favorite psychiatrist teacher/professors was fond of saying that to be a good psychiatrist, you must be able to hold mutually competing thoughts in your mind, and not feel compelled to resolve them. One should take the time to reflect upon the issues, and in time, a resolution— or at least comfort with the contradiction—will come.

Somehow, I am capable of holding in my mind contradictory points of view on the matter. I am horrified by abortion, yet I would never tell a woman what decision she should make about this. The government should be less involved, not more, in controlling the process. Phrases like "abortion should be safe, legal and rare" are helpful, but do not address the reality of the issue. The serenity prayer is always helpful. But in the end, there are situations that challenge any strongly held view of how the world is or should be ordered.

Exhaustion and Empathy

When the word spread among my friends and family that I had gained admission to medical school, I received many compliments, frequently with comments about how "smart" I must be. But exceptional brain power is not the primary factor in who earns the degree of Medical Doctor. By and large, most doctors are no "smarter" than other professionals, such as schoolteachers and mechanics. The basic concepts about how people get sick and then get well, or not, are not that complex. The difference is in the volume of information doctors must learn. The difference is stamina.

In my first year of medical school, we had a series of professors who presented lectures in the basics of their own specialties. They all came with armloads of paper handouts for each of us. I once asked a few of my peers, during a coffee break, how much of the handout reading they actually made it through.

"Maybe half..." one guy answered.

"Liar! Braggard!" another student jabbed at the first answer, "Maybe ten percent, at best."

Another joked, "But I'm saving all of the paper to build a cabin."

It's no surprise that the practice of medicine has evolved into specialty areas. Ten years into practice, not many psychiatrists can still read a complicated electrocardiogram. Ten years into practice, not many cardiologists can discuss the differential diagnosis of a patient who is hearing voices. The sum total of all information across all specialties is just too vast.

The issue of stamina came most personally to me during my fourth year, rotating as an "Acting Intern" on a neurology service. Acting internships are a kind of "jump start" on learning what it will be like in the first year beyond medical school, during the internship year.

The neurology rotation was a busy one, but up to a point that's good. One wants to see a lot of patients in order to gain experience of the real kind. During the on-call night, you want to have at least one new admission to the ward. Two admissions is a lot of work, but you still might get some sleep in the early hours before rounds, typically seven in the morning.

My first night on-call began with three complex and confusing admissions. I worked hard to evaluate each one to gain a general understanding of diagnosis, and what other diagnostic information

I needed to be confident in what I was thinking. I leaned pretty hard on my immediate supervisor, the junior resident on the ward. He didn't exactly scold me for how often I called him, but it was clear he was not used to being called by the intern so often. Let me be honest; he made me feel stupid. Real interns would have known more. For my last few questions, long after midnight, I did not care that he was irritated, I needed to know some things that I did not yet know. I was too exhausted to be embarrassed.

I stumbled back to the on-call room about 90 minutes before rounds. I told the hospital phone operator to give me a wake-up call in an hour. I figured if I could get just an hour cat-nap I'd survive. I lay down in the bed and noticed that my legs were aching. My fatigue was more than mental. I had been running from room to room and up and down stairs for twelve hours. Elevators take too much time, and besides, elevators are for wimps, according to the prevailing medical culture.

I immediately fell asleep. Ten minutes later, I found myself awake, standing outside the on-call room in my underwear, I looked back in the room and saw the phone receiver on the floor. I heard a faint voice calling out, "Doctor...are you there...doctor?"

I was called to the emergency room for my fourth admission. I put on my clothes and took time to wash my face. I took a half-dozen or so deep breaths, decided not to scream, and headed back down the stairwell. Maybe the patient would die before I got there.

The patient was a teenaged black girl who had suffered a stroke due to her sickle cell anemia. I forgot about being tired. I did my job. Late for rounds, I did not apologize. No one felt sorry for me, so I didn't either. This was the culture. Spend your time in the pit. This is something you need to learn. Be glad you're not the one in the bed.

I'm told the culture has changed for medical education today. It's not the macho experience it once was. Perhaps the change is because most medical students now are women. I am not suggesting they couldn't handle it. I am saying they helped change it. It is a good thing.

A similar experience happened when I was on overnight on call at a state psychiatric hospital. The patients just kept coming for admission, and several disturbances on the wards didn't make things any easier. Finally, my shift was over and I headed off to the on-call quarters to get a nap before seeing the patients on the ward to which I was assigned.

Walking past a patient room, I briefly looked inside and saw what I thought was the strangest looking man I had ever seen. He looked like a leprechaun, dressed in green wearing a pointed hat. A few steps past the room I stopped. I needed to know if we really had admitted the "Lucky Charms Cereal" mascot. I went into the room and found it empty. I even looked under the bed to see if someone was hiding there. Ultimately, I accepted that fatigue and exhaustion can lead to hallucinations.

Section Three

Joining the Profession

How Do You Learn How to Be a Psychiatrist?

Among those who try to understand human psychological functioning, there has long been a fundamental difference of opinion about how to even study this question. Simply put, at least in the 1970s, this was a conflict between the brain and the mind. "The brain is the organ of the mind" was and continues to be a commonly accepted concept, yet some argue for a primary focus on biological processes. Others argue that while biology is a necessary foundation, a true understanding comes from a study of the larger set of human experiences, especially human attachments.

For the most part, we beginning psychiatrists were protected from the raging conflicts and competitions surrounding the "canon" of psychiatric thought and theory. The UNC Department of Psychiatry's leaders at the time I began training, in 1975, were psychoanalysts (of the mind). Things were about to change, with new research into mental illness and biology (of the brain). New seemingly effective drugs especially for the more severe forms of mental illness were coming available, and theoretical assumptions were being challenged.

Perhaps more importantly, my years of training took place during the roll-out of the latest version of the psychiatric diagnostic "Bible," the *Diagnostic and Statistical Manual of Psychiatric Disorders*, version three, or *DSM-III*. The previous edition was a theory or causal based framework, often from a psychoanalytically driven point of view. The new version was created by a group of psychiatrists who started with the proposition that we do not know enough to say what causes mental illness. They created a "descriptive" nomenclature, proposing that more rigorous attention to criteria that separated one entity of mental illness from another would lead to clarity of causation, and more importantly, a clear focus on appropriate treatment. Avenues for true scientifically based research would follow.

It would not be an exaggeration to say that for the parties at war over causation and treatment, this was an existential struggle. Appointments within the academic world and funding for academic departments and professorships were at stake. And those of us still in training were not entirely protected from the fallout. One member of our resident class was essentially kicked out of a case conference by a psychoanalyst because the novice psychiatrist had used a "psychic poison" (a new medication) rather than continuing to try to treat the patient with psychoanalytically oriented psychotherapy.

A year or so later I would have my own version of being caught in the conflict. I had a patient diagnosed with obsessive compulsive disorder. I was trying to treat with psychoanalytically oriented psychotherapy, under the supervision of a psychiatrist considered to be a brilliant teacher. Everything he said about the patient, and what I should do, made perfect sense. The patient quit my treatment anyway, little improved, and sometime later the patient confronted me on the street in a chance encounter. She told me that her family doctor had prescribed a new medication for this disorder, resolving all symptoms. I got an earful about what a dope I was to not know the right thing to do to help people.

I don't want this to imply the analysts were always wrong. Psychodynamic psychotherapy has helped many people, and our profession would soon learn the limits of drug treatment. There were plenty of teachers over the years who overused and misused medications trying to use drugs when they were not helpful, and on occasion harmful. One faculty member was famous for suggesting electroconvulsive therapy for just about everything he encountered. Any symptom discovered was said to be a "depressive equivalent" and treated as such, usually electroconvulsive treatment. (*When the only tool you have is a hammer, everything looks like a nail.*)

And I don't want to make it sound like we were truly traumatized by this conflict between the choice of medication vs. psychotherapy. The learning environment I experienced was always stimulating and often inspirational. Nor do I want to say all professors were driven by a specific ideology. I once sought out one of my teachers for extra supervision focused on my puzzlement about several competing therapeutic models. He acknowledged that there was room for smart people to disagree. The fact that we reached no conclusions about most of what we discussed was in a real sense exhilarating. To not know something with certainty was liberating. To not be tied to dogma gave me a sense of freedom colored by humility.

In summary, a psychiatrist learns how to do this by reading research data, (there was and is some science available here, not enough) listening to those experienced in the profession, and "try this and see what happens." That's another way of saying trial and error, but we try not to use the word "error." More about that later. To put a positive spin, call it "experience."

The Patient as "Other"

Student doctors realize early that the medical disorders they are learning about could happen to them. The ability to manage this fear was not part of the formal curriculum, but I do recall several examples that shed light on the problem, both during medical school and in psychiatric training years.

Early in my training, an experienced urology professor concluded his presentation to my class of first-year medical students. "What you have just heard today is about the functioning of a healthy urinary bladder, and how pathology manifests in a distinct set of common symptoms. So, here is a question. How many of you sitting out there are considering showing up in my walk-in clinic for a consult just to be sure you don't have a serious problem?"

No hands went up, but I noticed that some students glanced around the room to see who might declare their worry. I saw a few smiles break out on the faces of my classmates.

"No takers? Well, what about this: how many of you are grateful we are now at a break so you can race to the bathroom to relieve yourselves?" Many smiles. He was on to us.

"And how many of you are reviewing the calculations in your head about how much urine the kidneys can make in an hour and are absolutely convinced there's no way you should need to empty your bladder now if you didn't have a serious problem?" He scanned the room to see if any of us would speak up. No one did. I heard a few chuckles.

He paused, giving us a wry smile as he took off his clip microphone, holding it in his hand, then continued, "Well, before you make a lot of unnecessary work for me in my clinic, just stop to think about how many cups of coffee you scarfed down this morning on your way here. If we counted, I think we would find about fifty empty cups on the floor in here."

Walking away from the lectern, he stepped closer to the auditorium seats to address us further. "You see, working up a slow-burn panic about how you must have some deadly condition is a well-known phenomenon in new medical students. Probably a quarter of you will develop the belief that you must be on some level suffering from one or more of the new pathologies you're hearing about. Male concern about the urinary bladder tops the list every year. My clinic seems to be where you show up to find out if you have something wrong."

Still no questions or comments came from the group, despite his frequent pauses and open hand gestures inviting dialogue. All the chuckles and smiles had stopped. He had a room filled with very attentive students.

"Now I am not saying you will never be sick. The other side of the coin is that some of you are likely to ignore real symptoms of an illness, thinking that just because you are a doctor you can't get sick. You are a doctor. You are not the patient. That can change. There's a little more than a hundred enrolled in your class. Statistically speaking, for people your age, you'll have one or two of you get really sick while you are here, with at least one of you having a psychotic break, or something close to it. You will not die, statistically speaking. But, again, before you go running to a doctor, use a little common sense. You won't likely have a third world parasite in your gut if you haven't been around third world people or been to a third world place. And if you suddenly believe you have an illness that you learned about only yesterday, pretty good chance you don't have it."

At this point the professor turned away from the group, put down his mic, gathered up his class notes, and put his long white coat back on. He left with one final comment. "Okay, I usually stay after class for questions, but if you are not going to ask me about this in front of your peers, I'm not hanging around for private consults. Besides, I need to get to the restroom before I pee on myself."

The problem of turning out to be the patient when one is trying to be the doctor can become even more of an issue with those who choose to pursue psychiatry. By the time I was two years into my psychiatry training I had learned the lesson that some psychiatric disorders can be seen as extremes of common human emotions, such as anxiety and depression. It is the rare individual who has not had some experience of stress and sadness, and it is often unclear when such experiences justify a diagnosis and call for extraordinary attention, which we call "treatment."

Complicating the issue is the fact that some people who pursue a career in psychiatry are motivated to do so because of emotional challenges they experienced themselves or witnessed in their families. The question frequently posed and considered is whether having the experience of suffering psychiatric symptoms—or perhaps growing up in a dysfunctional family—makes a person a better psychiatrist. The intellectual answer is it should not matter.

The training undertaken in order to become a psychiatrist, and sometimes treatment that a psychiatrist may receive as a patient, should help delineate the boundary between who is the patient and who is the doctor. Ultimate comfort and confidence come through clearly defined roles. However, this effort to create useful boundaries does not always go well, as illustrated in the following case conference.

A resident psychiatrist in his third year of training, the last year before graduation, summed up a case chosen for an educational conference. As lead presenter, he spoke in a small room filled with students, perhaps a dozen learners, of various levels of training. He spoke with an air of authority and confidence, although with stiff formality. "This thirty-four-year-old mother of three simply has not met the emotional needs of her son and daughters, and the consequences are clear. It's clear she has failed in the fundamental tasks of nurturing and structuring in the lives of her children. None of the kids are learning up to potential in school, and the youngest one has regressed from being fully potty trained. The mother seems preoccupied with her own needs and is more focused on her own mother's dysfunctional life than the life of her children. This all came to a crisis when she unwisely decided to start dating again, even though the court case about her ex-husband was still unresolved. I think we need to really consider a referral to child protective services and see if these kids are better off in foster care."

A student social worker, most likely the youngest person in the room, quickly joined the discussion. "I don't agree at all. You've been seeing one of the kids, but I've been working with this woman for six months now and she's made real progress." The social work student's face showed multiple emotions, mostly anger, as she pleaded, "I think she has been a hero to her children and should get a lot of credit for what she has accomplished. Things are so much better for everyone now. I really admire her."

Surprise showed on the resident's face. "Really? She's made a real mess of her life. Lot of really bad decisions."

The student responded, "Well, the bad decision she made was to marry a rich psychopath and have three kids with him. But I think she's done a great job for her kids in the last few years."

The resident gave the student a patronizing smile and leaned back in his chair, arms folded across his chest, as he responded, "So, you really don't think she's doing anything wrong?"

"With what she's had to deal with...the physical abuse...of her and the kids...the man's infidelity to her, and the way he's spent his money to drag her into court again and again. I don't see mistakes on her part so much as her just trying to survive. I mean I don't think I could have handled her situation any better than she did."

A chuckle preceded the senior resident's remark, "I think you're over-identifying with your patient a bit. Be careful about keeping your boundaries strong. Do you really think you would have gotten yourself into this kind of mess? She's missed every opportunity to get her life to a better place and...well, I don't see much but a lot of poor decisions made by a person without a lot of emotional strength and maturity. She's obviously got a lot of holes in her psyche."

At that point the senior psychiatrist and supervisor of the conference interrupted, softly addressing her remarks to the resident. "I think you're being a little hard on your colleague there. One does have to keep in mind who is patient and who is the therapist, but putting yourself in the shoes of another is a good way to understand and not blame..."

"Blame the victim! *Not* blame the victim!" The student social worker exploded back in, squirming in her seat, gesturing with her hands. I wondered if she was getting ready to walk out or come across the table at the resident who still wore a smirk on his face. "Every step along the way, this woman gets blamed for everything that's gone wrong in her life! A team of lawyers have tried to label her as crazy...in court! The...the police were always on the ex-husband's side until they saw how he beat her up one time! And now you think she should have her kids taken away? Make her the bad person...and punish her! The kids have been through hell and back...and their mother is the only constant in their lives...and she's made sacrifice after sacrifice! That's ridiculous! You're just wrong about this...you're blind! Maybe if somebody is identifying with someone else it's you identifying with her husband." She ended her retort by raising herself up in her chair and looking the resident straight in the eye. He looked stunned and remained silent.

The supervisor of the conference restored order by praising the work of the student social worker and agreeing with her take on the situation. Therapy would continue as before. No referral would be made to social services. The resident kept silent and did not comment further on the specifics of the case. Instead, looking up at the ceiling, he ultimately began a somewhat detached monologue about something he had read about family therapy, quoting from a book by a well-known family therapist.

The supervisor gently interrupted, "Yes, those are all good ideas to consider, but right now I'm going to call us back to the cases we have to discuss. I think we are done with this one…who's next."

As we all went our separate ways after the conference, I reflected on the interaction between the social work student and the resident. It occurred to me that he may have held to a fundamental belief that a person is always responsible for the trouble that visits them. A mentally healthy person would never allow life to get so out of control. In that view of things, it would be bad decisions that should be the key focus of therapy. I wondered if he believed that certainly nothing so bad would ever disrupt his own life. He would never be a victim. He was not a patient and believed he would never be one.

Unsung Heroes

During my first year of psychiatric training, I sat beside a much older man, who I'll call James, in the day room of the state psychiatric ward, awaiting the arrival of a dozen or so patients for a social skills group. James was a Health Care Technician, called an "orderly" by some, that name reflecting a previous nomenclature.

"We never could have had a group like this back when I first started here." He smiled as he spoke, and I sensed he had more to say to me, a novice, still in my training years. My facial expression must have conveyed my interest, so he continued. "And I never had a moment to sit, like this. Always a fight to break up, a spill to clean up, or someone to take in or out of seclusion."

"How long ago was that?"

"I started here right after getting out of the army, 1946."

I knew enough to understand he was talking about the time before even the first generation of antipsychotic medications, but I simply smiled and nodded. He clearly wanted to tell me a story.

"I'll never forget the first time I saw them use Thorazine. There was this big, ornery guy, thought everyone was trying to kill him and his only way out was to attack. He spent most of his time in seclusion. Most of that time tied down. Ate like a starving sailor. Pooped on the floor. Or on himself. Took five of us to give him a bath using a hose." James chuckled, shaking his head from side to side. I was entranced by the story and by the man telling it.

"So, when the doctors here got their hands on some Thorazine, he was the first one here that got it. I can't remember if it was shots at that point or, somehow, they got him to swallow it. And a day or two after he was taking it, I came in for a three-to-eleven shift and the nurse told me to go into the seclusion room. The man wanted to ask me a question." By this time, James was laughing and slapping his knee, clearly enjoying the attention I was paying him.

"I asked the nurse if he was tied down, and she just motioned with her hand to go on down the hallway. I knew something was up, and then I saw that the door to the seclusion room was open. I swear you could'a knocked me over with a celery stalk when I looked in the room. There he was, just sittin' on the big restraining bed, in street clothes, clean shaved, and with a brand-new haircut!"

I made a few remarks about how unusual it was for antipsychotics to work that quickly, probably trying to tell the storyteller that I did know a little about all this, but he did not comment. He ended his story that the man spent all of the previous day asking people what were their names. James came up with the idea about why the man was so interested in names, that the man was simply trying to "find his place in a new reality." One of the doctors liked the phrase that James coined and started using it in case conferences for patients who are getting better on the drug. The doctor took credit for coming up with the words of the phrase.

Our conversation was interrupted by the current patients filing into the room. The social skills session, led by two registered nurses, was generally uneventful. I could see it was rewarding and helpful for some of the patients. I also noticed that by the end of the meeting, patients were directing most of their comments and some questions not to the nurses, but to the "orderly." James had a presence in the room that I did not fully understand, but patients were drawn to his demeanor. I struggled to name it: maybe maturity, maybe wisdom.

I spent as much time around James as I could, but hampered by the busyness of the ward routine, I heard only one more real story. We sat for a few minutes in the staff break room and he talked about treatments before drugs were available.

"Shock treatment was rough in those days. A lot of people got it just to calm them down. It worked pretty good for that. And back then they got no medicine, not like today where they get put to sleep before they're zapped."

I was already familiar with the modern form of electroconvulsive therapy, that treatment having evolved as appropriate for only the most intractable depression and psychosis. Patients received both a general anesthetic and a powerful drug to relax the muscles so no one would have to restrain them like in previous times.

James continued my education, "You had these strong leather restraints on them and several people holding them down so the seizure wouldn't have them flailing about. They could break an arm if you didn't hold them right. A really strong seizure by a big guy could actually pop a strap, but you couldn't hold 'em too tight or they could still pull muscles, or dislocate a shoulder, or break a bone. One of my first jobs was to lie crossways across their legs, since I'm kind of a big guy. You had to learn how to hold 'em steady but let 'em rock a little."

I wish there had been more time for history lessons, but the orderly was not the only unlikely hero I encountered. In a different hospital, at the medical center in Chapel Hill, I served a four-month rotation on a ward run by a nurse who I will call Phillip. He was a man who was considered wise and experienced beyond his formal R.N. degree. The official leader in the medical chain of command was the "Attending" Psychiatrist, but Phillip had earned the trust of this psychiatrist who granted him de facto authority beyond that of the head nurses on the two other psychiatric floors of the hospital. The psychiatrist said more than once that Phillip could easily pass the exam given by the Board of Psychiatry. He made it clear that we student psychiatrists should listen to Phillip.

Still, we newbie psychiatrists were collectively skeptical about Phillip's talents and status, and we openly talked within our small group about our reluctance to defer judgement and authority to a mere "nurse." I changed my mind the first week. A situation with a violent patient introduced me to some things I did not yet know and showed me what kind of skills Phillip had.

The patient in question had received a death sentence due to cancer and was admitted to the psychiatric ward after a suicide attempt. While already ravaged by the effects of his malignancy, he remained a large, heavy-set, robust man...and an angry one. Among the injuries and insults to his mind, body, and soul was the loss of an arm.

The metal prosthesis with which he was fitted was not exactly a "pirate's hook," but such devices at that time were still primitive compared to today. The part metal, part wood device displayed visible wires and screws, with the hand portion made up of a simple "pincher" function, terminating in a curved point sharp enough to serve as a weapon.

I had guided him through a week of hospitalization, focused on grief, anxiety management, and good health habits including staying sober. He reached what appeared to be a sad but peaceful and accepting state of mind and took the lead in developing a list of practical things he needed to get done before he died. Because he seemed serious and diligent in what he was trying to accomplish, I wrote him a weekend pass. He went home to get started on his tasks and we agreed that if things went well, he would return that Monday as a formality and be officially discharged.

When I walked onto the ward Monday morning I could tell from the quiet and anxious tone on the ward that something was not right. The ward secretary motioned to me immediately, "Mr. (so and so) is in his room and says he has to talk to you right now."

As I turned to walk down the hall to his room, Phillip appeared out of nowhere, walking beside me. We passed two large, male Health Care Tech staff leaning unobtrusively against the wall halfway to the patient's room. Phillip addressed me, "It's your call Dr. Bridges, but several of the staff are very uncomfortable with the condition he came back in. He looks intoxicated and he may need to spend a little time in seclusion for detox."

I opened the door to the room, not sure what I would find. I felt uncertain about how to handle what was clearly a difficult situation, and further unsure about how my interaction with Phillip would unfold. I knew the Attending Psychiatrist would not be on the ward for several hours.

We were two steps inside the room when the disheveled, red-faced, and angry patient stood up out of a chair and yelled at me, "It's about Goddammed time you got here. I'm ready to get the fuck out of here." His wife sat tearful and obviously afraid on the side of the bed, the area around her eye clearly blackened and red from some kind of recent injury. The man held his arms rigidly down by his side. My gaze went directly to the hook.

He continued without pause, "I shoulda never let her talk me into comin' back here. It's a fuckin' waste of time to be here. I was just fine at home, but no…she kept whinin' and cryin' that I needed to come and check out." He turned to his wife and said "And I'll deal with you later."

I was speechless. I had no idea how to calm the obviously intoxicated and out of control man. Phillip rescued me. "Dr. Bridges, let's go back to the nurses' station and get some paperwork ready. See if we can get this man on his way." We stepped outside the room and closed the door behind us. There were now four male staff gathered right outside the door. Phillip turned to me and simply raised his eyebrows. I said, "I think he needs seclusion." I'm sure Phillip saw the deer-in-the-headlights look on my face as I meekly nodded.

"I'll take that as a doctor's order," Phillip said conclusively.

Phillip turned, spoke and gestured quickly to the four men, "Okay, I've got the hook. You two on the legs, you on his good arm, and you get his head. And let's be tight on this. I won't be lookin' at anything but the hook, but I don't want to get punched, kicked, or bit. Ready?" He turned to me and said, "You stay back. Poke your head in the door and watch if you can get a good view."

Phillip was not a big man. No one would have mistaken him for an athlete. But he led the four other men into the room in a quick and efficiently choreographed operation. He walked directly to the patient and used both hands to grasp his prosthesis; he put his shoulder hard into the man's chest, knocking him backwards into his chair. Almost immediately the others scrambled into the fray and soon had both legs, his other arm, and his head tightly grasped and under control. He gave up without a fight. Phillip quickly removed the prosthetic arm, the hook, and the four others carried him down the hallway to the seclusion room. Elapsed time: three minutes.

After he was safely confined, I stood just outside the room with Phillip and the man's wife who cried tears of relief. She was led away by a nurse to a private office. Phillip turned to me and said, "Well, that went okay, you think?" I agreed and he turned away with a comment, "Let's go do that paperwork now."

I soon realized that all of this could have happened without me being there. The staff had "standing orders" for seclusion that could have been initiated by the nurse in charge. It occurred to me that Phillip had let this unfold as part of my education, but this was never openly discussed. The other thing that was never talked about again was any doubt about Phillip's judgement or skills, or any questioning of his authority.

Perhaps I was predisposed to learn from those not quite at the top of the pecking order, because the earliest "hero" I remember from a medical setting was a nurse. When I was in college I worked at a local hospital as an orderly to pay for my education. The assistant director of nursing was a woman recently retired from the military but young enough to start a new career path in the civilian world. All business, confident in her skills and authority, she still managed to have a sense of humor. I'll call her Ms. Smith.

Much of my orientation, my on-the-job training, came by following her around for the better part of two weeks. One of my duties involved moving patients in their beds to and from surgery. Ms. Smith and I worked together on the admission for a sixty-plus year-old minister who was in for a procedure in the area of his private parts, probably an inguinal hernia repair. I helped settle him into his room the previous afternoon in preparation for the procedure. I remember thinking that he looked like a Norman Rockwell version of a grandfather. Arriving at the hospital dressed in a vested suit, he carried himself with soft-spoken grace and politeness.

Finished with surgery, awake after several medically uneventful hours in the recovery room, the man was ready to be returned to his room. Ms. Smith and I wheeled him down the corridor on a stretcher. But the minister displayed an unusual state of mind. He spoke gleefully and expansively, and loudly, to all around him, announcing that his surgery was successful. His exact words were "Hooray, hooray, they just fixed my ping-a-ling ding. My ping-a-ling, my ping-a-ling, my ping-a-ling ding!" His previously regal demeanor was gone, replaced by the face of a gleeful child.

I learned later that he had been given a new drug for surgical anesthesia, one that did not ultimately pass the test for widespread use because of unusual central nervous system effects in some patients. These unusual effects in this gracious man culminated in a memorable scene, as follows: in the middle of a busy hallway leading to his room, Ms. Smith and I pushing the bed as fast as safety allowed, the man enthusiastically waved a towel above his head as if he were at a football game, and repeated loud and long that his ping-a-ling ding had been fixed. His desperate wife shuffled along by the side of the bed trying to put her hands over his mouth.

Finally situated in his room, intravenous fluid bottle affixed in the proper manner, he calmed a bit, but continued to smile and to embarrass his wife. Ms. Smith closed the door and turned her attention to her patient. She gently took the hand of his wife away from his mouth, and held it in her right hand as she then placed her left hand on his shoulder.

After a short pause, she looked directly in his eyes and in a matter-of-fact tone, she spoke. "Yes sir. It is indeed the truth that we have fixed your ping-a-ling ding. No question about it. And everyone here is very, very pleased that we know how to do that kind of surgery here. And now everyone who needs to know that we have done this is now informed that we did it. So, we do not need to talk about it anymore."

The man looked startled that she had spoken to him in this way. He then became very quiet and, as far as I know, for the duration of his hospital stay, never spoke of it again.

My second adventure with Ms. Smith took place in a taxicab. The emergency room took the call from the taxi dispatcher who announced in an anxious voice, "They're in the cab and they're headed your way...the baby's halfway out!"

As a crew of about six staff stood outside the emergency room door, Ms. Smith took care to tell us to hang back and stay safely out of the way of the taxicab as it careened up the driveway, horn honking non-stop.

"Bridges! You come right behind me! The rest of you stay back unless I call you."

I followed a step behind as Ms. Smith yanked open the back door of the cab, first helping a young man roll out and fall on the ground before she entered. My memory is not clear about what I first saw, some blood, a crying woman, but mostly Ms. Smith's back as she did whatever it was that she was doing.

"Okay Bridges. Step up here close and I'm gonna hand you the baby! Hold out both your hands. It's slick, so don't drop it!" She looked past my shoulder and barked at the others, "Other side! Other door! I need those instruments, now!"

As the other staff raced to the far door of the car to assist from that side, Ms. Smith plopped a screaming, bloody, wet infant into my hands. "You're not a fainter, are you, Bridges? You damn well better not throw up!"

At that point I did not have a clear understanding of the relationship between baby, umbilical cord, placenta, etc. So, I can't really describe what happened next. I didn't faint, fall down, or throw up. I did my job of not dropping the baby until someone came and took it out of my hands, wrapping it in a warm blanket.

Ms. Smith later praised me and said she knew I could handle it. I told her I played football in high school and I just pretended that I was catching a forward pass. That wasn't really true, but it sounded like a good thing to say. We both agreed that it would be a good story that I would tell for a long time. I'm still telling it, and other stories about Ms. Smith, fifty-plus years later.

Fallen Heroes

In my second year of training, I had a number of experiences that showed all my mentors and models did not walk on water. Beginning my rounds on the hospital psychiatric ward in Chapel Hill, I flipped through the paper chart for the patient in room 404. Reading his name, age, address, and reason for admission, I did a doubletake on his stated profession: physician/psychiatrist. Surprised that someone from my chosen profession would be hospitalized on this ward, I read carefully the notes about how he came to be here. His recent history sounded—for lack of a better word—ordinary. Up to that point in my training, all of my psychiatrist teachers and role models still wore their halos. This kind of fall from grace should have been—for lack of a better word—more extraordinary.

I interviewed him, reviewing with him his admission story: heavy use of alcohol, domestic conflict with accusations of violent behavior, and a possible charge of resisting a police officer. He confirmed the basic information. All of the problems had one thing in common: none of this was actually his fault.

One of the things I asked about was his work, "I don't actually have information here about where you work and what kinds of problems you're having there."

"That's not something you need to worry about," he barked at me. "I'm in private practice…and my office secretary is contacting all my patients to say I'm out for a week…with an illness. That's all taken care of…I'm fine there."

He broke a short silence by pointing at his bruised upper cheek, gently rubbing his eye with the back of his hand. "Looks pretty bad, huh…she knocked the hell out of me." Another pause. "I hope I didn't hurt her…don't remember much…" Tears formed in his eyes. He sobbed briefly, then wiped his eyes and stared past me with a blank look on his face.

Unsure of how to address the issues he presented, especially whether there was more to be said about his work situation, I focused on his physical health and the orders for his detox from alcohol. I felt a growing awareness that I needed to get to my supervisor and sort out how to think about and approach this patient.

Overall, working with the hospitalized psychiatrist proved both illuminating and puzzling to me. My supervisor stifled more than one chuckle at my naiveté about the personal vulnerabilities of members of the profession. No one, except me, was surprised when he went through detox uneventfully, convinced all involved to drop the legal charges, and returned to his private practice less than a week after his admission. I suggested perhaps the medical board should be notified about his struggles, but no one else thought it was needed.

That experience did prepare me for a related event almost a year later when I moved from inpatient work to outpatient-clinic work. I had been assigned a supervisor who worked part time for the university and part time in private practice. I traveled a short distance across town to meet with him in his private office.

At our first meeting he greeted me enthusiastically, but somehow without making eye contact. His gaze jumped around the room and he took a moment to look outside in the hallway before we began. Finally, he gestured to a large chair in the room. "Have a seat, and if you don't mind, I'm going to stand by the window while we talk."

This struck me as unusual, but I complied and took my seat in a large leather armchair. He stared out the window as if I were not there. I took the lead. "So, I've got a list of new patients, just got it this morning…and I've seen only one of them, so, I guess we should talk about him…or…how should we use our time today?"

He responded, mainly to himself, as he continued to stare out the window and said, "I think my car is on fire." He invited me to come over to the window and see if I saw smoke coming from under his car. He still had not actually made eye contact with me.

I walked to the window but saw no smoke from his car and told him so. He continued, "I have a gun and some bullets in the trunk, so if it's on fire I need to go get them out." I agreed with him that this was important and he should take care of it promptly. I walked out the door as fast as I could as he continued to look out the window at his car.

Driving directly back to the training center and going immediately to the director of the outpatient clinic, I reported what

I had experienced. He mused, "Hmmm...well he has had a lot of personal problems over the last few years, but he's really a brilliant guy...I think you'd learn a lot from him...what do you think we should do?"

"I want a new supervisor! That's what I think we should do."

"Really? You don't think you can still work something out with him? I think he'd be a really good supervisor.

"But he's hallucinating that his car is on fire and he has guns and bullets in his trunk! Why does he think he needs to have guns in his car?"

The clinic director paused, then spoke reflectively, "Hmm... that's a long story as I understand it, but I don't think in the long run..."

"I am not going back. The man's crazy!"

After a little more back and forth, he assigned me a new supervisor for my outpatient clinic work. The new one, along with two others for the outpatient year, collectively provided some of the best learning experiences of my training.

There is a postscript to the problematic supervisor experience. I attended a dinner party later that year where conversation led to my relating some of my experiences as a psychiatrist in training. A young woman who I met for the first time at the party asked me if I had ever had any dealings with a certain psychiatrist, who turned out to be my troubled supervisor. Choosing discretion, I answered only that I knew of him.

She commented, "Well, he's something else. I tried to go see him for therapy, but he kept calling me up in the middle of the night and sobbing into the phone. Wasn't really helpful to me. Didn't really work out."

My third year in the training program brought another challenging situation. Perhaps I should have been better prepared, however, this time there was a personal element. I was assigned to a one day per week rotation at a community clinic. This rotation was designed to introduce me to the real-world, beyond the world of the university training center.

In what turned out to be unfortunate timing, my first two weeks at the new site came when the psychiatrist clinic director, my assigned supervisor, was on vacation. Nevertheless, I spent those two days of the rotation introducing myself to the other staff and felt good about how I might fit in. Several of the clinical staff asked me to provide some in-service education and we set this up for a mutually convenient time.

When the psychiatrist supervisor returned, he greeted me as I entered the building for my third day at the clinic, "So...you must be Dr. Bridges. Come with me and we will interview a patient."

I wasn't sure how to read this first interaction, but I didn't feel good about it. I followed him down the hall and into an interviewing room. He introduced himself to a young, black man who was stylishly dressed and had spiky, orange colored hair. He addressed the patient. "I am the clinic director, and this is my student. I am going to interview you and my student will remain silent. Why are you here?"

The young man hesitated before he answered, clearly on-guard due to the curt way he was approached, then replied, "Uh...having some relationship problems."

"Relationships. Okay. I think I see. You're homosexual, right?"

"Uh...yes..."

"So, what is it. You're maybe having problems pleasing your boyfriends, yes, is that it?"

"Not really..." The young man's discomfort clearly grew as he squirmed in his seat, frowning.

"Okay, so you're good at pleasing the other boys. So, what is it? What is the problem?"

I felt the need to do something about what I thought was a very inappropriate and insulting interview, but I had been told to stay silent. To my surprise, the patient continued to answer the questions.

"The problem is with my family..."

"Of course, it is," the psychiatrist said condescendingly, "they threw you out when they found out you were...uh...what did they call you; did they call you queer, perverted...?"

"No, it's not that at all. They are fine with all that. The problem is they want me to move back home and...and...take care of them. They're broke and sick, and, and..."

"And you're busy pleasing all your boyfriends and can't make any room for them."

I wanted to scream at the psychiatrist. I didn't want to simply leave; I was embarrassed that he would treat someone who came for help in what I thought was a hateful way. But I sat there for about half an hour and just listened to what I thought was psychological torture.

Nevertheless, as the interview progressed, the young man became increasingly assertive, but polite. He ultimately described his life as one of learning how to be a survivor and the most capable member of a severely dysfunctional family. The psychiatrist surprised me with his final comments as he ended the session, "You don't need to come here. Just go ahead and live the life you have. You don't need anything from us."

With the patient gone, the psychiatrist turned to me and asked, "So what do you think?"

"Well, I think I might have approached him in a different..."

My supervisor jumped to a standing position directly in front of me. "You think! You think! You would do something different from me! Who do you think you are? You come into my clinic and set up these training sessions with my staff before you even ask me!"

I was stunned. I wanted to run but he was between me and the door. I sat silently, preparing myself to fight or flee, as he continued his rant. "So, I guess you come into my clinic as an expert, wanting to train my staff. Tell me, what are you an expert in?"

"Well...I don't think I'm an expert in any particular thing...but I have learned a..."

"Stop! Let's see what you have learned. Define anxiety, please."

I began a traditional definition of anxiety having to do with internal psychological conflict and he interrupted me again by holding up both hands and turning his head away from me.

"Stop! What about the spiritual definition of anxiety, and the existential definition of anxiety, and the moral definition of anxiety? You have so much to learn...here...I have a few books for you to read and if you can present me with a useful discussion of anxiety from a cultural and spiritual point of view, then maybe I let you try to teach my staff."

He turned his back on me and began rummaging around in his bookcase. When he turned back around, he found himself alone. I left quietly and made my way back to the overall supervisor for this part of the training program. He reassigned me elsewhere. At that new location I met a man who became one of my very best friends for the next 40 years. Had I not walked out of the first location, I would never have met him.

The best example of finding something valuable in an uncomfortable situation came late in my training years. Two female faculty members in the training program had sponsored a "feminist writer" as a guest for the department's Grand Rounds educational series. This took place in the late 1970s, a decade of growing cultural conflict about the Equal Rights Amendment and the rise of the National Organization of Women (NOW). TIME magazine had named "American Women" as their "Man of the Year." In 1973 tennis star Billie Jean King and Bobby Riggs staged their "Battle of the Sexes" tennis match.

The Grand Rounds presentation was sufficiently interesting—and provocative—that several of the men in our residency class approached the women faculty members about offering an in-house series on "women's issues." (We men already considered ourselves as generally "enlightened" about such issues and we believed our willingness to ask for this experience proved just that.)

Viewed in the lens of today, the content of the series was very tame and modest. Topics such as equal pay for equal work, the absence of women in leadership positions, and other assumptions about gender roles were explored. However, a few subcurrents emerged. In addition to the otherwise thoughtful and timely issues that formed the core of the experience, the women faculty members seemed to use the men in the group (who were all residents/students) as surrogates for their anger about their mistreatment by the male dominated leadership of the psychiatric training program.

The other men and I soon realized that we were stuck in the middle of culture war. This became even more clear because of what we were otherwise hearing from the male faculty members. The attitudes of the men faculty toward the women seemed to range from mild disdain and patronizing tolerance to outright hostility. Many were not shy about expressing it.

One example of such attitudes is illustrative. The outside feminist speaker at Grand Rounds had used the term "consciousness raising" in reference to an approach to women patients who presented with symptoms of depression. Later, in a small group lecture series, a male psychoanalyst was asked about the term. He replied, "Consciousness raising? Consciousness raising? We've been doing consciousness raising for a long time. Here's how you do it. Take your right hand and grab the left ear. Take the left hand and grab the right ear. Then you jerk! If that doesn't expand the mind a little bit, then nothing will."

It became clear what these women faculty members were experiencing in their professional lives. The only time I felt personally bruised came from the fact that one of the women teachers never missed a chance to make fun of my southern accent during the sessions. I always simply smiled and acted as if it were no problem. I guess I was doing the same thing they were doing in the face of a perceived power imbalance, remaining silent.

That last experience came in the final months of my training. As I faced graduation in the near future, I appreciated that the flawed teachers had taught me as much as any of them. I walked the halls of the training program with the floors now littered with bits of broken halos. I felt comforted by the realization that I did not have to be perfect to move on to what was next.

Section Four

On My Own

Continuing Education

I now had finished the last of the formal schooling necessary to work as a physician/psychiatrist. My education consisted of four years in a medical school and three years in a psychiatric training program. Both had the best of reputations. Now, I faced the task of creating a practice that earned me a living. I felt well prepared in the basic medical knowledge to take the next step, but less confident about where and how to turn this into an income generating situation. Lofty ambitions for accomplishment and acclaim took a distant back seat to the need to make money.

Still undecided about how I wanted to spend the majority of my professional time, I chose several part-time options. I rented office space and spread the word that I was accepting patients. Beyond that, in order to earn at least some money right away, I signed on for a two day per week job at a rural community mental health center. I wasn't that excited about working there, but I learned that a lot of new graduates did this kind of work until they built the kind of practice they really wanted. To my surprise, this rural clinic became a place and time of invaluable and unexpected new learning for me.

Before seeing patients in this clinic, I toured several facilities and programs run by this county and state funded entity. I began by visiting what is generically called a "psychosocial rehabilitation program" for those who suffer from severe and persistent mental disorders. The director of the program, a late thirties year old man named John, welcomed me into the house where the program was located. I was surprised to discover the house was a very impressive five thousand square foot, two storied, hundred -year-old Victorian style mansion. This house was located in an area of town that was no longer a "desirable location" and had stood empty until the mental health program leased it for this program.

We took seats in large comfortable wing chairs in a space that was nothing less than a well-appointed upper-class living room. John's energy and enthusiasm for his work and his program came with his first words. "We don't call people patients here, they are members. They come here not to be taken care of, but to get things done. And we don't give ourselves a fancy name. We're just the adult day program, or ADP for short."

Getting things done was immediately on display. I could hear the clanking and clinking of a busy kitchen just two rooms away from where we sat and talked. Through a large picture window, I could see several men and women outside loading lawn mowers onto a small flat-bed trailer hitched to a full-sized pickup truck.

"Do you have a lawn service where you live?" John asked me. "We travel about an hour in all directions. We're not the cheapest service on the market, just the best."

My preconceptions of what I would find at this program were already upended. I had expected a much more passive place, where patients were cared for paternalistically, or perhaps maternalistically. The right word might have been "sheltered." But John and I were the only inert figures in this frame. The surprises were just beginning. I started to ask about the house, but a more pressing concern interrupted us.

A young man walked into the room and directed a comment to John. "Lenny's back."

John sighed, then smiled. "So, he's back. Are we surprised? What does he want?"

"He wants to come back. He says he's sorry."

John took a deep breath and asked, "What kind of shape is he in?"

"Not good. Smells bad. I've seen worse. He's not injured. Says people have been throwing rocks at him near the water tower."

"Oh God, here we go again. Where is he?" John rolled his eyes.

"I put him in the big bathroom."

John looked at me with a twinkle in his eye, "You're here at a good time, you get to see what we do here. Follow me." Together we walked to a relatively private area at the back of the house that had been renovated into a larger, spacious modern bathroom. Through the open door I could see a tall skinny man wearing a band uniform. His long and disheveled hair was colored a combination of yellow and purple.

John spoke to him. "Lenny! What in the hell are you wearing? You look like shit!"

I turned to look at John, shocked by the way he was talking to a "patient." Nothing in my knowledge base or skill set suggested this was an appropriate way to interact with the man.

John continued, "Lenny, you stink. I can't believe what you're wearing and how bad you smell! Have you been marching again? I guess so. But you know what happens when you dress up like a crazy man and go marching around town. Did anybody hurt you?"

Lenny looked up at John with a meek smile and response. "No. I'm okay. So, can I come back here?"

"If you let me clean you up and get you some decent clothes."

"Sure," Lenny said.

I sat in the hallway, and over the next half-hour, listened to John put Lenny in the shower and shampoo the yellow and purple color out of his long hair. I walked down the hall with John and watched him open a large well-stocked walk-in closet and pick out new clothes for Lenny.

By the time Lenny was scrubbed and casually but appropriately dressed, lunch was served to approximately twenty staff and members before they headed out to various activities. We sat around a large ornate dining room table, flanked on two sides with ornate wallpaper depicting a pastoral scene. People came and went, some ate quickly, others lingered to participate in a follow up discussion I had with John. Lenny had left with the lawn crew.

John smiled at me and asked, "Have you figured out who at lunch was staff and who were members?"

Several of those who stayed behind smiled but did not speak. I had not been trying to figure this out, but with his prompting, I reflected on who looked the most "normal" at lunch and who engaged in conversation. I realized I had no confidence in my assessment. No one was behaving as a "staff" versus a "member" as far as I could tell. Everyone in the room had participated in the preparing and the sharing of the meal, no one seemed to give orders, and no one acted strangely.

"Don't try to guess," John added, "You'd be wrong."

As I was leaving, with only the two of us in conversation, I asked a question I thought might be helpful and relevant, "With Lenny, it's pretty clear he's not taking any medicine, I mean, is that right, and are you going to help him work on his compliance with his meds?"

"That's not our job. We don't concern ourselves with what they take or don't take. That happens over at the clinic."

"But it's clear to me that he needs something. He's probably hearing voices or some kind of intrusive thoughts," I pressed.

John spoke softly and patiently. "That's probably true, and he'll get around to figuring it out. Maybe you'll be the one to see him over at the clinic, but here, at the day program, we have a different focus. We don't talk about voices and visions and things like that. We let people know what is and is not normal behavior...about the things you might do to get people to run away from you, dogs bark at you, or have people throw rocks at you, or call you names, or worse. We try to get people to learn how to act to be a part of real life."

As I drove away from the day program, I had many questions that I didn't ask. Do the members get paid for mowing the lawns? Is there a risk of violence if the staff doesn't pay attention to the members taking medications for psychotic disorders? Can a person just show up and join? Is there no application and acceptance process?

From there, I drove to the clinic where I would get my next dose of reality education. I was hired there to take over the case load of a retiring psychiatrist, a much older man who had worked at the clinic for many years. What I learned from taking over his case load of patients took a while to unfold.

In my first week in the clinic, I saw many patients with complex, multiple diagnoses and who were taking what I thought were unusual combinations of medicines. This did not fit with the current thinking of those who taught me in the training program. My best teachers had advised something that could be summarized as follows: "make one diagnosis and treat with one drug." I was surprised that things were not done that way here. My first impression was that the senior psychiatrist who was taking care of these patients seemed hopelessly out of touch with the modern approach. So, I set about to make things right.

In the first weeks and months of my work in the clinic I reduced the doses and discontinued many medications when I thought the patient was overmedicated. More than a few of the patients asked me to not change their medication. Some clinic staff advised against what I was doing, but I took pride in the belief that I was bringing modern psychiatric medicine to needy and underserved rural patients, and to an uninformed clinic staff. My confidence was shaken when a significant number of these patients regressed; their symptoms such as hallucinations and depression returned in full measure. Some went back to the hospital. I reluctantly concluded that *some of this stuff they don't teach you in school.*

Starting a Private Practice

Office rented, furniture delivered, and various forms of paperwork organized, I opened my office in Raleigh for the business of seeing private patients. Some would have medical insurance coverage; some would pay cash. I had made visits or phone calls to other psychiatrists already in practice in the area, and I kept in touch with people in the training program from which I had just graduated. My practice location was less than an hour from where I trained.

Referrals trickled in slowly, but one day after only a few weeks, I found myself with six people scheduled on a single day. All were repeat customers. I remember thinking that this was going to work out, despite my lingering self-doubt about being ready to be on my own, not to mention my minimal understanding of fundamental business processes. I was still blushing about embarrassing myself during the process of getting my office telephone ordered and installed. Reading from the installation receipt, I asked the man who was connecting the phone what the words "auth per tele" meant. He did not hold back his audible chuckle as he defined it for me. It was not the last time I displayed my naivete about business processes and terminology.

Perhaps unsurprisingly, that first day with a full schedule did not begin well. The first three patients did not show up. No cancellations or calls to reschedule, just nothing. When the fourth patient did arrive, his first words were "I've decided that I don't really need this, so today will be my last appointment."

I stifled my urge to leap across the room, take him by the collar with both hands and scream "Like hell it will be your last appointment, I have to earn a living here, fool!"

He did pay me what he owed me before he left, so I did at least have enough to go to lunch and put gas in the car. I allowed myself to be optimistic that the two people I had scheduled in the afternoon would show up.

I felt a sense of relief when the first scheduled afternoon patient did indeed arrive. He was a middle-aged man with multiple mental and physical problems. Half-way through the session, things took another twist. He suffered a grand mal seizure in his chair right in front of me. Fortunately, he was accompanied by his wife who helped me attend to him. As he regained consciousness, she reassured me that he would be okay, that this sort of seizure happened at least weekly, and all he required now was to get back home and rest. No ambulance was needed.

As he stood to leave, I noticed that he had wet his pants. The chair was a plush, cloth covered one, with a soft cushion seat. The seat was wet. He apologized profusely for wetting the chair as his wife helped him out the door.

I was hardly concerned about a soiled chair cushion. It was easy enough to have it cleaned, but I did realize that I now had another problem. My final patient of the day, an older "delicate-little-old-lady" loved that chair. At each of her several previous appointments she commented on how comfortable it felt and she joked about buying it from me. She was due to arrive at any moment.

I considered my options and chose to flip the cushion over. No way the wetness could soak all the way through to the other side. When she arrived, I greeted her in the usual way, and she went immediately to the chair she loved. She sat down hard in the seat and proceeded to bounce up and down a few times to get comfortable. I felt panic. She wore a lacy, fluffy flower print dress.

The session felt like the longest hour I had yet experienced as a psychiatrist. I did not hear a word she said during the entire appointment. I kept looking at the edges of her frock and with every change in her facial expression, I expected her to cry out that her seat was wet or ask what was that awful smell?

When the session came to an end, she reached for her purse to pay me. I interrupted her with "Uh...I have a new policy...you can pay monthly...so we're done for today." I did not add what I was thinking: *get the hell out of that chair before I have my own seizure!*

Now alone in the room, I stepped over to inspect the cushion. Totally dry. I collapsed into the chair just to celebrate my escape from my stupidity, and just to double check that I felt no wetness on my own pants.

Staying Safe in This Profession

More than a decade into my forty-year work life as a psychiatrist, I sat in the conference room of a rural mental health center eating lunch. I now worked full time in this clinic that provided care for all who sought our services, regardless of ability to pay. The May 1992 newspaper on the table in front of me featured multiple stories about what would come to be known as the "Rodney King beating." Riots had broken out in Los Angeles in reaction to an acquittal of police offers accused of excessive force in the apprehension of a 26-year-old Black man.

I read the paper with an eye to whether or not the story had mental health implications. A long car chase had ended in what was said to be a brutal beating of a drunken man by multiple officers. I knew that mentally ill people sometimes hurt other people and that just as often they became the victims of harm at the hands of others. I wondered if this situation was mostly about alcohol or something more complicated.

My lunch was interrupted by Ron, the staff member on call. "When you're finished, doc, I'll tell you about the man the police are bringing in."

"Go ahead, I'm done."

"This one's a real mess. We been gettin' calls all morning from the family of a man they say is out of control. Said they couldn't get the police to come out, even though he's been breakin' out windows in houses and cars since the sun came up."

"What's that about?" I asked.

Ron looked down at the newspaper I was reading, pointed to the article about the riots, and said, "Not sure. It might be about that."

Ron explained that the patient I would be evaluating was a young Black man who was in a rage in his own neighborhood, smashing windows, jumping up and down on cars, and threatening anyone who came near him. He had a long mental health history, and we had a thick chart on him. The police were called but said they were having trouble freeing up officers from other duties to respond. It would later come out that the only officers available to respond were white. Given the images on the news of the last few days, the dispatcher was not going to send white officers to restrain a black man.

Within the hour we stood just inside the back door of the clinic, watching through the glass door, as the man in question was carried up the walkway toward us. He was young, muscular, and fighting as hard as he could, carried by five black men, each holding on to one of his arms or legs, and the fifth trying to control his head. He spit, cursed, and tried to bite those who carried him. Walking a respectful distance behind the group was a single small, skinny, white police officer who carried the legal papers.

We subsequently learned that the men who carried him were cousins and neighbors. Absent police response, these men organized their own group to restrain him. Police ultimately arrived and placed handcuffs and leg restraints on him, but told the five men they needed to continue to keep hands on him.

Ron and I held the door open as they carried their charge inside. All of the men had torn clothes, scratches on their arms and faces, and looked exhausted. I led them to the room where involuntary commitment evaluations were conducted. After they were ushered inside this mostly empty twelve-by-twelve-foot room, I stood just outside the door with the policeman and read the legal papers that were a part of the commitment process.

Once satisfied that the papers were in order, I stepped just inside the door. The five men lay sprawled on the floor beside or on top of the agitated man, several speaking softly to him, offering reassurance that no one was going to hurt him. One of the men looked up at me and barked, "Well, motherfucker, are you going to come on in and do your fuckin' job!"

Realizing that my personal safety depended on five exhausted men who were clearly furious at the lack of help they were getting from the authorities, I looked at him and said softly, "I think I have enough information to finish my part. This will not take long."

Thus, ended the shortest involuntary commitment evaluation in the history of psychiatry. Within ten minutes, the entire group was again in the police van and on the road to the state hospital.

The above story stands in contrast to a pair of other incidents concerning potentially dangerous patients. The first happened just days after the above incident and involved a man brought in on emergency involuntary commitment papers. He was said to be assaulting a neighbor "while in a blind alcoholic rage." Police protocol called for such patients to be in handcuffs and leg irons. We received a phone call that he was on the way. I and the emergency services staff prepared ourselves for another possibly difficult experience.

I felt surprised and a bit uneasy when I watched the police bring the man in through the back door. Not only did the person in custody not have on any restraints, but the officer in charge had his arm around his shoulder and was talking to him in a friendly way. Before I could speak to share my concerns, the officer said, "This is John, he's my wife's cousin. He's been a little upset, but he's okay now."

Early in the exam, I came to agree with the officer. The story in brief: two buddies started drinking too early in the day and got in a fight over something. I can't remember if the fight was over a woman, money, or a football team, but it was something of that nature. The other party lost the fight but was the only one of the two capable of finding his way to the local magistrate's office to file the papers for commitment.

I found this man to be a sad, confused, and remorseful—yes, intoxicated—person who just wanted to go home and sleep. The officer said his shift was ending and he promised to go with his cousin-by-marriage and stay with him the rest of the day, overnight if needed.

Yet another version of danger from a mentally ill person started with the sound of broken glass and the sight of staff running down the hallway. A middle-aged woman had let herself in the unlocked back door and went in search of a particular staff member. She believed that one of our staff members had a part in the removal of her children from her home by the child protective services unit of the Division of Social Services. Unable to find her primary target, she moved from office to office and proceeded to randomly smash against the wall any item small enough to throw.

Armed with some training about how to de-escalate explosive situations, I stepped forward to confront the woman in the hall. I pulled up the words I was taught might be successful in engaging enraged people. "Wait, wait...let me help you here. I'm on your side."

These so-called "magic words" designed to define oneself as a helper and not an adversary, did have the effect of stopping her for the moment. She looked at me with a puzzled expression, so I continued. "I can see you're upset...but I think I can work with you to get what you want." I said this with more hope than conviction. This woman showed a range of emotions in a single moment: fear, anger, and confusion. She had tears in her eyes.

I assumed, correctly, that in another part of the clinic the call had been made to the police. But for now, I assumed a non-threatening posture, head lowered, arms folded across my chest, showing my hands held no weapons, keeping a respectful distance away from her. She accepted my invitation to talk about what had upset her. For several minutes she poured out her story of the loss of her children, then asked me a question.

"So, you'll try to get my kids back?"

"I'll do everything I can. I really want to help."

At that moment, two police officers came rushing through the back door toward us. Glancing over her shoulder she seemed to understand what was happening. Unfortunately for me, she no longer considered me to be "on her side." I had betrayed her. She stepped forward and aimed a kick at my groin. I moved aside just enough to catch the kick on my thigh. Her fist glanced harmlessly off the top of my head. I slumped against the wall as the police restrained her. She was dragged kicking and yelling from the clinic.

I and our clinic learned a lot that day about being prepared for these kinds of situations. Locks were installed on the back doors. Our clinic staff openly mourned the loss of innocence of our open door, friendly little clinic. Dangerous people were supposed to arrive in tow of law enforcement. A few months later, as the large red and blue bruise faded from my leg, I enrolled in a martial arts school.

Several years later, we were still a small clinic and choices of doctors remained limited. I found the woman who kicked me on my schedule. She was taking her medicine for her mania and had her kids back.

At first, there was no acknowledgement of our prior encounter, but later in the session, she asked, "Are you the doctor I tried to hit."

"Yes, that was me."

"I hope I didn't hurt you."

"No problem. I'm fine."

Medical Mistakes and Malpractice

I stood outside the seclusion room for the psychiatric ward of a small community hospital, my first stop on morning rounds. Looking through the eight by eight-inch reinforced plexiglass window into the room, I had a clear view of the patient who had been admitted at 3:00 AM that morning on an emergency petition. The head nurse began her review of the patient's last several hours.

"The Haldol prn doses, two in total, finally seemed to calm her down a bit so we let her out of restraints, but we kept the bandages on her hands because we weren't sure she wouldn't start punching the window again. We need to get a good look at her hands soon. Looks like nothing is broken but lots of blood from her knuckles."

The viewing window was not the only target of her fists over the last 24 hours. Earlier, she had assaulted several friends and family, but the most impressive punches were directed to the police officers who brought her in.

The nurse continued. "Otherwise, she seems to be in good shape physically. I got a pretty good look at her body. She wouldn't keep any clothes on for the first few hours she was here. So, I don't see any injuries, but doing a physical on her will be a challenge. To tell the truth, I'm impressed with the restraint by the police. She messed up a few of them pretty bad. But I don't think they hurt her back."

Now fifteen years out of my training and having worked in various settings, I had seen many such agitated and almost certainly psychotic patients. I went through a mental list of possible diagnoses, from mania to drug induced, and reviewed with the nurse a sequence of steps we needed to take, including drawing blood for lab tests and drug screens.

I was pleasantly surprised when the nurse said, "We're a step ahead of you there. I had a feeling that while she was still in restraints, we could draw some blood. Got the whole panel, including a tube for a drug screen. Lab downstairs is holding off on the drug screen 'til you call and say what you want."

The patient, twenty-seven years old, probably six feet tall and well over two hundred pounds, finally saw me looking through the glass and approached the window. Her emotionless expression turned to screaming laughter and she pressed her lips and tongue against the glass in a caricature of a sustained, watery kiss. She soon lost interest in us and meandered around the fifteen-by-twelve-foot room, empty except for the heavy restraining bed anchored to the floor, adorned only by a bare mattress.

An hour later, I had finished the rounds and turned my attention to various paperwork. The ward clerk handed me the readout of our new patient's lab results. Most of it was unremarkable, but one value caught my eye, an assay of an enzyme, creatinine phosphokinase, or CPK. This enzyme is found in various organs, heart, liver, muscle, and in the normal state stays inside the cells of the appropriate tissues. If found in high concentrations in the blood stream, that's big trouble.

Her CPK read 19,000. "That comma must be a period," I muttered, mostly to myself. Nobody has a CPK of 19,000. I called the lab. They couldn't believe it either. They ran it three times. It was real. The findings suggested serious destruction of some kind of cells within her body.

I knew of one condition, rare but well-known to psychiatrists, called neuroleptic malignant syndrome, or NMS, that could be the reason for her elevated enzyme. Haldol, a drug for psychosis and agitation, had been known to cause this sometimes-lethal condition. But patients I had known with this condition had high fevers, delirious if not comatose, and certainly were not walking around. I organized a small troupe of nurses and male aides and we entered the room to examine her, and draw more blood to repeat the lab assay. She cooperated with minimal restraint. At first, she did not speak. There was no fever, no neurologic symptoms that I could discern from a minimally cooperative patient, indeed, no abnormal physical findings.

As we were leaving the room, she smiled and spoke softly to me. "I love you. Will you save a dance for me?"

"Not right now," I said. We left. She waltzed alone, with a big smile on her face.

This was all playing out in a small rural hospital on a brand-new psychiatric ward not yet fully integrated into the medical services of the larger hospital. I had worried about how we would handle complex medical emergencies. I had known we would eventually face just such a problem. I didn't expect it to be our ninth admission. But I knew I had at least one ally on the general medical staff, so I called him immediately. He listened carefully and talked me through a list of possibilities. Then he said "This isn't something we can handle here. I don't think anyone here has ever seen NMS, if that's what it is. I'll be happy to look at her, but we always send these kinds of patients to Duke."

I retreated to the privacy of our conference room and over the next half-hour made a series of unsuccessful calls to Duke Medical Center. The doctors with whom I talked showed poorly disguised dismissive attitudes toward me and told me in no uncertain terms that I should not send the patient. No room in that hospital for such a patient.

I had one other option. I knew that Dorothea Dix Hospital in Raleigh operated a general medical unit within that larger psychiatric facility. I called there, but the staff member on-call for that unit, a nurse-practitioner, seemed confused by what I was asking and said she'd have her physician supervisor call me back.

I responded to a knock on my door, from the head nurse who had taken over for the day shift. "I think you need to look at this." She handed me the written report of the lab studies we had just ordered for the patient. "The guy down in the lab said he had never seen anything like this."

The CPK read 39,000. I felt bewildered. I knew you didn't treat lab values, but nothing fit together for anything for me to do. While I waited for the return phone call from Dorothea Dix, we went back in to examine the patient, and again took her temperature. She now had a fever of one hundred and one degrees. And she was still dancing, and offering to kiss anyone who would kiss her.

Back in the conference room, waiting for the return call, I felt panic. I was afraid this woman was getting ready to die on me, and no one would help. Finally, the phone rang. The call-back came from Dorothea Dix in the person of a recent graduate from the psychiatric training program I attended. I knew him a little, and he recognized my name. He also happened to be a rising "star" within the profession and would eventually rise to national prominence for his research and organizational leadership. After brief pleasantries, I explained my problem.

"Don't send her here," he said, "it's not an appropriate admission."

Without pause, I exploded, "I'm sending her now! I suggest you meet the ambulance in the parking lot. You can turn it around and send it back, and we'll let the lawyers decide who gets the blame for her death!"

Fortunately, the local ambulance services did not challenge my authority. She left within the hour. And Dorothea Dix medical unit decided to admit my patient. Over the next twenty-four hours I kept in touch with those in charge of her care. They gave her no additional medicine at first. Apparently, the effect of the Haldol she had previously received eventually calmed her, and her CPK and her fever started to fall.

The doctor in charge of her case opined, "I don't know why she had those abnormal labs, but she certainly does not have NMS." He communicated willingly with me, but running through his reports was a less than overt message to me that I had over reacted and all this drama was unnecessary. Pretty "routine" kind of case.

Unfortunately, her agitation and psychosis soon grew worse. Still in the Dix medical unit, she received a single injection of a drug similar to Haldol. Within half an hour she experienced a grand-mal seizure and went into a coma that lasted several weeks. Ultimately, she was taken by helicopter to the medical intensive care unit in North Carolina Memorial Hospital. My last conversation with the doctor at Dorothea Dix featured a little more respect for what I was dealing with and how I had handled it.

She recovered completely from the effects of NMS, and ultimately returned to see me for an appointment at the local out-patient clinic. I saw no psychiatric symptoms. She didn't remember any of her experiences, even the dancing, and did not return for follow-up appointments.

One year later I signed for a registered letter that came to me at the clinic. In everyday terms, it was a malpractice accusation. For those who have never looked at such an accusation, it is brutal. In short, I had allegedly failed to diagnose and treat the patient consistent with how any other competent physician would have known to do. The accusation's legal verbiage is written in such a way that had you done the things of which you are accused, you should not only be sued, you should be shot. I thought I had been her hero.

The above situation stands in contrast with the times I did make medical mistakes, but did not get sued for my shortcomings. The most serious of my mistakes was with a 90 plus year old man, a farmer, a man who had literally never been to a doctor in his entire life.

"Can you just give him something, doctor?" was the request coming from his granddaughter, who explained he had become confused, angry, and aggressive at bedtime.

"He thinks we are trying to play tricks on him. He says that's not his bed and not his house." Further information revealed he refused to go to a hospital and the only reason he agreed to come to see me was that his granddaughter worked in the same facility where I worked.

I gave the traditional reply, "No. I can't do that without a real workup. At the very least we need some lab tests."

His granddaughter broke down crying. "You just don't know what we've been through! I've been up most nights this week with him, trying to get him to go to a doctor. You'd have to tie him down to stick a needle in him. And I'm not going to call the police on him and see him taken away in handcuffs!"

This interview took place in the early part of the day. No signs of aggression at that time in my patient, but it was clear he was only marginally understanding what was being discussed. He asked no questions. My best diagnosis with the information I had was that this is a frequent problem among the elderly. Apparent cognitive decline, confused and aggressive at the end of the day, all pointed to a primary dementia.

Physically, this was a very healthy-looking man. I remember thinking that I could only hope I would look that good at 90. Even with no real exam, I could see he had no swelling of his legs, no trouble breathing, no jaundice of his eyes, and he sat with good posture and no signs of pain or distress. And then I made the mistake. I agreed to treat him with a very low dose of the medication used for aggression in patients with dementia. No lab studies ordered.

The patient and his granddaughter returned to see me later that week. "Doctor, you have hit the nail on the head. He's had the best two nights of sleep in months. And me too," reported the granddaughter. I smiled, relieved, and repeated that somehow, we needed to get him a real medical checkup. They both agreed and said they would schedule with her family doctor as soon as they could get an appointment.

One week later, I received a message that my patient was in the hospital at a regional medical center. He had suffered a seizure and was rushed there by ambulance. Finally getting a full medical workup, he was found to have a parathyroid tumor. The tumor was removed and the man returned home with no medication and his problems with aggression resolved.

Waiting for them to follow up with me for one last time, I focused on the fact that a simple lab screening test would have identified a metabolic abnormality that pointed toward the correct diagnosis. I braced for the worst from the family. What I received was only gratitude.

"We really want to thank you for working with us. My grandfather says you are a fine man and he likes you a lot. You're the first doctor he ever saw and if he knew they were all like you he wouldn't have waited so long."

All doctors make mistakes. Some can be egregious and fatal. Some are "only" uncomfortable. The mistakes in judgement that I am aware of making usually came with patients with complex general medical conditions. Not all drug side effects that patients experience are known until the drugs are in use with the real-world population. Some patients take so many drugs that drug interactions are bewilderingly complex.

Even without mistakes in judgement, the drugs that psychiatrists have to treat patients often have harmful effects along with helpful ones. I once was referred an elderly woman with a drug induced medical condition called tardive dyskinesia. The muscles of her mouth and throat were compromised to the point that she needed a feeding tube for nutrition. The general physician who had been treating her for almost four decades decided that she had become too complicated for a family doctor.

On my first meeting with the woman and her husband I wondered if they might be inclined to bring a lawsuit. Did they even know the drug had caused the condition? I wondered about my duty to explain how and why she developed this neurological condition. Would I become an expert witness in a lawsuit against the other physician?

What the family told me was that the anti-psychotic drug she was taking enabled her to leave a ten year stay in the state hospital and return to her family and four minor children. They called the drug a miracle. I was allowed to reduce the dosage, but if I had stopped it, I doubt they would have come back.

I was cleared of the malpractice claim brought by the dancing woman. In the other case, I'm not sure I would have won if the man and his granddaughter had filed one. Fortunately, he didn't die. The lesson learned is that malpractice claims are sometimes brought against doctors who have performed well and done no harm. Also, genuine mistakes do not always generate malpractice claims. Why? The variable is the quality of the relationship between the doctor and the patient. Patients can forgive mistakes if they believe you were doing your honest best, even if you were wrong.

It Is What It Is, But It's Not What You Think

A few minutes late coming from an administrative meeting, I rushed into the small rural outpatient clinic where I had an afternoon of patients waiting. Hurrying through the half-filled waiting room I did take note of two police officers in uniform seated side by side. Their presence almost certainly meant an emergency involuntary commitment evaluation was waiting for me, making the typically busy afternoon for the clinic even more packed.

A staff member approached me and said, "Your one o'clock appointment cancelled, so you can take care of the commitment first, if you want to." Mary, the appointments and medical records staff member, walked with me down the hall to my office. She handed me the legal papers for the emergency petition. "And his sister is already in your office. I tried to tell her to wait, but she insisted that she needed to talk to you first. She wouldn't take no for an answer."

Now at the door to my office, I looked inside to see a stylishly dressed and made-up fortyish woman, who stood immediately and spoke to me. "I sorry if I'm out of line," she began, "but I came here all the way from Boston when I finally figured out the fix my brother had gotten himself into. I seem to be the only one who is upset about it." I motioned toward a chair with an open palm for her to sit. I asked her to tell me what she had learned about her brother.

"I had no idea how he was living until I had a conversation with my uncle, who told me he was living all by himself in our parents' old house. They died a few years back. He's mentally retarded and totally unable to take care of himself. And when I got there, I freaked. There's no food in the house. Almost no furniture. There's a bed and a chair or two and that's about it. I have no idea what happened to our parents' furniture. Somebody stole it or maybe talked him into selling it for nothin'. It's just a big mess."

"How long since you've been down to see him, before today?"

"It's probably been ten years, maybe more, but listen, I know him really well. I'm six years older than he is. He's almost forty, and I helped raise him, and took care of him, 'til I moved away. He's still got lots of family around and I thought they would be taking care of him, but this is unbelievable. I'm angry about it!" She seemed close to tears.

"What else can you tell me about how he lives? And what do you know about his general health?"

"I don't know about his health, but you haven't heard the really messed up part. So, I looked around in his house and he has all these police uniforms and he tells me he's a cop. Ridiculous! He has the mind of a five-year-old! So, I went next door to a neighbor—not the same people I knew when I lived here—and I asked them about the house and the police uniforms. You wouldn't believe what they told me. He gets up every day and puts on this stupid police uniform and goes marching around town pretending he's a policeman. He's gonna get shot or something!"

"Have there been any incidents... of danger... or violence that you know about?"

"How would I know that! I just got off the plane this morning. But I know he's crazy and he needs to be put in some kind of home or something that will take care of him and get rid of those stupid uniforms! He needs to be in a facility!"

"Did you see any weapons? Guns? Other things like knives?"

"I didn't see a gun. And the fact is, no knives, not even a fork or spoon. How does he eat?"

I quickly reviewed the papers that had been filled out by the local magistrate ordering him to be brought for an exam. The sister was listed as the petitioner and no other names appeared on the documents. The written information was essentially what his sister had just told me. I told her I needed to examine him myself. I excused her from the room.

Retracing my steps to the waiting room, I remembered thinking there were two officers seated, but obviously one was the officer, and one was the patient. Viewing them again, I saw two very well dressed and groomed men. Were it not for the fact that one wore a gun and other police equipment on his belt, I would have been hard pressed to guess who was the subject of the exam.

The actual officer stood quickly and spoke, "Doc? Could I speak with you for a minute? Before you do your exam?"

The standard procedure for those brought for a commitment exam was that the person in custody be handcuffed, for the protection of everyone. But no cuffs here, except the ones on the officer's belt. I started to ask the officer if he was comfortable leaving his charge unattended in the waiting room, but he walked briskly past me, and I followed, pointing ahead to the appropriate room.

"Doc, this is a big misunderstanding. There's no problem here. This is all so unnecessary."

I briefly reviewed the concerns presented by the sister, but the officer interrupted me before I was done. "Doc, there's no food in the house because he eats two meals a day at somebody's house in the neighborhood. A late breakfast and supper. Everybody takes turns, probably ten or so families have kind of, like, you know, adopted him, if you get my drift. It's either that first next-door neighbor, or a brother, that helps him put his check in the bank and helps him get what he needs. Helps him pay his light bill and water and all. It's not really much of a check. Lots of people put an extra dollar or two in his pocket. He couldn't buy what the people in this neighborhood do for him. Actually, you couldn't find people anywhere that do for him what they do."

"What about the police uniforms? And does he think he's a real policeman?"

The officer smiled and leaned back in his seat. "Well, this all started before I was on the force, but way I understand it, about ten years ago he was wandering around the town, looking in people's houses, and so the police keep gettin' calls, but somebody figured out he was harmless and came up with a plan. They gave him a job to do. Patrol the neighborhood."

"And he gets the uniforms from?"

"From us. Give him the ones we have that are getting' a little too much wear, but still look good enough."

"Are you not worried...?"

"Only thing I'm worried about is that sister that comes runnin' back from wherever she lives and messes up something that's good for everybody. We check in on him once a day, just in the course of what we do, to see if he's seen anything unusual in the neighborhood. Tells us about people he doesn't recognize. He knows his job is just to look and tell somebody if he's worried about something. No trouble ever with him."

"So, you think it's a good situation?"

"It's a great plan, doc. I can tell you more...when it gets really cold, he's got a few families that either check on him to make sure he's got heat or even take him in overnight. I can give you a couple of phone numbers of people who will tell you the same thing. I think most of them know his routine. Where he'll be at ten, at two, and so on."

As required, I examined the patient alone. I later documented that his only mental condition appeared to be a low IQ, that I guesstimated at about fifty. And although it was not necessary for me to comment on this, I wrote "With the right kind of help, you can do a lot with an IQ of fifty."

I released him from legal detainment into the custody of the officer, who stated that he would now take him to the man's brother's house, who was part of the support system. When I informed the sister, she turned without speaking and left. As for how the plan worked out, I continued in that clinic for close to two decades and heard nothing from anyone about this man, his family, or his neighborhood.

The situation with the "community policeman" is not the only such situation I encountered. It concerned a teenage girl who we knew well from early in her life. She had experienced little else than chaos, abuse, and neglect in her family. We had made some progress in helping her and her family, but she had disappeared from our services. This was not good news. Gaps in her treatment always ended in crisis. Our staff member assigned to her had reached out to other agencies, private professionals, and all social service and legal programs to find her. We assumed that her "notoriety" within the community guaranteed that if anyone had news of her it would be shared, confidentiality about information sharing notwithstanding. No information was available.

In the midst of a busy morning, the clinic's emergency services staff knocked on my door announcing, "You won't believe who just walked in, doc. June's back." I knew immediately who he meant and asked cautiously what kind of shape she was in. I expected another horror story of what she might have been through since she had been away from treatment for close to a year.

"It's not like you think, doc. She's in pretty good shape, actually."

"Do we know where she's been?"

Ron flashed me a big smile and said, "I'll let you get that story yourself, if you have time to see her. We're pretty slammed in the back. So, I'll let her minister tell you the story."

"Her minister?" I replied as the staff member left to attend to other emergencies.

I made time to see her. I reacted with equal measure of surprise to the two people who walked into my office. First, I truly did not recognize June. The last time I saw her she had a shaved head and a lot of metal in her ears, nose, lips and eyebrows. She stood before me now in a long blue skirt and white blouse covered by a navy blazer. Her blond hair was braided with two neat pigtails that reached just below her shoulders. No metal, except for the shiny clasps on her polished black shoes covering white socks that reached up just above her ankles. Two words came to mind: healthy and wholesome, words I would never have associated with June.

Her companion was equally notable. He was a tall Black man with a physique that suggested professional athlete, football or basketball. He wore a three-piece grey suit and sported a short afro haircut. Large rings graced four fingers of the hand with which he reached out to greet me.

"I am Deacon Johnson, and I am so happy you are able to see us. June told me nice things about you."

His giant hand seemed to swallow mine, as I returned his greeting and thanked him for bringing her in. I told both of them we had been worried about her and wondering where she was living.

My mind raced with questions. Deacon Johnson took the lead in defining the situation. "June has been living with Sister Sheraline, and she has been doing so well. We are so proud of her. She's a member of our church family now and might just be our smartest student in our home school. But June keeps asking us to bring her back to you for some medicine. She just doesn't sleep at night and has really bad dreams. Mean dreams, bad things happening to her. She says there was a medicine that you used to give her that would help her."

At this point I was fighting my own bad faith assumptions about the situation in which June now lived. While I had no information that suggested June was being exploited, I knew of more than one situation of mentally ill people being taken advantage of by "false prophets." I couldn't keep the word "cult" from coming into my mind.

The interview continued and I heard reassuring information about where June was getting her general health-care. I knew the doctor that she named. The home school sounded like it had a legitimate connection to the local county system. June even had a paying job at a local store, stocking shelves and occasionally running a cash register several hours a week, which gave her spending money. She was especially proud that she earned real money and was able to keep it.

Even with all the positive information, I concluded that I needed to talk to her in private. All this seemed too good to be true. Alone, June continued with positive comments. I asked open ended questions about how she liked where she was living, but I was careful to not suggest anything negative. Fifteen minutes into the interview, I asked if there were any problems she wanted to talk about other than the bad dreams. A frown came over her face and she looked down and paused. She then looked up and spoke slowly. "Well, there is this one thing."

My negative assumptions and suspicions returned, "So, there is something you are not completely comfortable with?"

"My magazines. I used to like to read *Seventeen* and *People.* But Sister Sheraline says they are not Godly magazines. And she took them away. And she does go through my stuff every now and then to make sure I don't read stuff that's not Godly."

I was able to respond with empathetic comments about how this must be disappointing and how it wouldn't be too many years until she is an adult and can make decisions like that for herself, but I was thrilled to hear that this was the worst thing about her current situation.

I wrote her a prescription for the medication that seemed to have helped her in the past. As I said goodbye to her and Deacon Johnson, I reflected on the fact that the mental health program had provided many hours of professional care for this sixteen-year-old from the time she was a toddler. We had not come close to accomplishing for her what this community of support had done.

I subsequently learned that the church in question had among its members many who worked in the local county school system, law enforcement, and social service programs. They took Christian charity seriously by reaching out to those in need.

Examples of how the efforts of people in the real world accomplished more for "patients" than we of the mental health profession were not isolated incidents. An older teen boy had bedeviled his family and community with his violent, borderline-criminal behavior fueled by alcohol and other drugs for several years. Short stays in jails and psychiatric hospitals did nothing for him and he seldom attended appointments at the outpatient clinic. Both during the day and after hours, our clinic took more than weekly phone calls about him, the general message being, "You got to do something about that boy!"

Then the calls suddenly stopped. At first, we were relieved, then puzzled. A few offered the idea that he must have died or moved away. We called around to people we knew in law enforcement and other community organizations. No one knew any more than we did.

Several years passed before the mystery was solved. One of our staff took his car to a small body shop for repair and came face to face with the missing boy, now a young man. He sported an appropriately soiled uniform with the business logo displayed on his shirt. Both men recognized the other and our former untreatable patient told the story of how he turned his life around.

It was all about cars, and the older man who owned the business who took a chance on the young man. His new life centered around Alcoholics Anonymous and his acquired gift for making a broken car look and run like new. He lived in a one room apartment above the shop.

One final example: another man had the same adolescent and early adult disaster of a life, then we stopped hearing about him for close to two decades. His savior was heavy machinery. Somebody put him on a tractor, then a backhoe, and eventually a heavy grader. We heard the story from the man's brother, who from time to time needed a little help for himself. Our "patient" who caused so much pain to self and others, eventually became a master in control of the red dirt universe. As long as he sat astride several hundred horsepower on four or more wheels, the world made sense to him.

Experience Does Not Always Make Things Clear

Adventures in Medical Ethics

After a few years of working in the profession, if things go well, options for "leadership" roles may present. I accepted one of these opportunities, to join the slate of officers for the North Carolina Psychiatric Association, the state advocacy organization for psychiatrists and their patients. I served as president of the organization in 2004 and traveled to New York City for the annual meeting of the American Psychiatric Association, to represent the North Carolina chapter.

I felt a little overwhelmed by the size of the gathering. Few locales can handle an invasion of 25,000 psychiatrists from all over the world. The meeting moves between cities like NYC, San Francisco, Washington DC, and Toronto on a rotating basis. This gathering also brings out the anti-psychiatry groups who regularly demonstrate against we-who-would-control-their-minds. I made a point of seeking out and anonymously moving around within the demonstrators to see what they were like. I found a combination of serious-minded critics as well as "colorful" characters. I couldn't stop from laughing when a mid-sized panel truck drove by with a printed sign that read "THE PSYCHIATRISTS ARE COMING— HIDE YOUR CHILDREN."

However, the most bizarre experience came inside a meeting of my peers. Our local organization's designated leader for ethical issues could not attend this meeting, so despite the fact that ethics was not an area of professional expertise for me, I attended this gathering of state and national ethics leaders. Several cases were reviewed by the group, to pass judgement on whether particular psychiatrists were rightly or wrongly sanctioned by their local organization. The overall point was to discuss general guidelines for the profession as a whole related to ethical boundaries.

The first case involved the issue of psychiatrists accepting gifts from patients. A child psychoanalyst had received a letter of reprimand. Her membership in the local state organization was placed on probationary status for accepting a gift from a child patient. While I certainly knew of and agreed with the rationale behind the prohibition of accepting gifts from patients, I was surprised to hear that the gift being discussed was a thank you card from the child patient, upon completion of therapy. The card was described in some detail, purchased from a Hallmark shop and enhanced with colorful heart-shaped stickers, the total value of the gift totaling less than five dollars.

I resisted my you've-got-to-be-kidding-me impulse and simply listened. The leaders of this discussion, all men except for one woman, all much older than me, talked at length about the damage done to the treatment by this gift. One even suggested that the psychoanalyst contact the child's parents and recommend that the child return to treatment, with a different analyst, of course, to address the harm done. There was no dissenting opinion. I made a note to myself to find someone back home to talk with about this.

The second case involved a psychiatrist who was treating a husband and wife for marital problems. In the course of the treatment, the psychiatrist separated from his wife and began a romantic relationship with the woman of the couple he was treating. She then moved in with the psychiatrist and divorced her husband. The husband brought a lawsuit against the psychiatrist and petitioned both the local medical board and the psychiatrist's professional organization for redress. The local professional organization began an ethics investigation against the psychiatrist—and subsequently dropped the case when the psychiatrist and his former patient married.

A final decision reflected the policy that "our profession does not involve itself in the marital relationships of its members." That seemed to be the end of the discussion. There was no information about whether the lawsuit or the state medical board investigation continued.

I was stunned by what I was hearing. I cautiously raised my hand, and although I can't quote the words I actually used, I expressed that something was out of balance. A therapist gets sanctioned for accepting a thank you card and another gets a pass for marrying his patient? The room went dead silent. You would have thought that I had confessed to killing Kennedy.

After a half minute or so of silence, a tall older man with a scruffy goatee, and a scruffier head of white hair, spoke loudly, "Well, if you want to totally abandon a deontological framework and throw yourself in with the teleological morass, I guess you could go down that road!"

Not fully conversant at that point with the terms he used, I sat silent as his colleague picked up the argument, "We've looked at utilitarianism as an option, but the real question here is are we going to have rules that are clear and consistent or not."

I wasn't sure if he was agreeing or not with me, so I pulled inward, just wanting to not be the focus of the question. I succeeded. One by one several others chimed in with comments generally incomprehensible to me, but no one looked at me anymore. For another fifteen minutes lofty phrases and urgent pronouncements followed. At length, the first man gestured with open palms to the group as a whole, "Anyone else?"

I ultimately familiarized myself with the terms they used. I vowed to never allow philosophical acrobatics to cloud my mind. I concluded I would be better served by the things I learned in little league baseball.

As an aside, regarding the issue of gifts, when I worked in a rural mental health center, I had a farmer patient who each year at harvest time would bring me a "big mess of beets." Once a year I cooked borscht.

I often think about something else that happened at another annual meeting of the American Psychiatric Association, this time in Washington DC. My hotel room was ten or so blocks from the site of the convention, so each morning I would walk to the meetings. I passed under several bridges where groups of homeless people had set up makeshift tents and beds. Even though it was early May, several mornings were uncharacteristically chilly. Small groups of the homeless huddled on top of heating grates. I reflected on what I had learned about mentally ill people within the larger population of the homeless. They gathered here halfway between the US Capitol Building and the national office of the American Psychiatric Association.

One evening during the conference, my wife and nine-year-old daughter and I went out for dinner at a Chinese restaurant. Our table was piled high with rice and the various dishes we ordered. When asked if we wanted the leftovers boxed up, I initially said no, then I had what I thought was a brilliant idea. I turned to my wife and daughter and said, "Why don't we box it up and take it to some of the homeless people?"

My wife smiled. "That's a great idea."

My daughter spoke with a stunned look on her face. "What? You people are nuts!"

We had access to our car at the hotel, so despite the protests from our child, we soon drove around the city looking for an appropriate person or persons to give what was easily three or four dinners with rice. My daughter kept up her verbal assessment of her parents' mental condition.

Giving away food was not that easy. Most of the groups we passed on the street at night seemed like they might just be people who wanted the car, too. So, we kept driving and finally we spotted a lone guy digging into a dumpster, having already made a small pile of items including what looked like McDonald's burger bags.

"There." I said as I pulled the car to the curb just around the corner from the dumpster. My daughter unbuckled her seatbelt and dove to the floor in the back seat. I quickly approached the man and held out the food, "Hey man, you like Chinese food?"

In the days following I would tell this story to friends. I sometimes waited before completing the story to ask them what they thought the man said to my offer. Many of my friends, some of whom were mental health professionals, guessed that the man turned down my offer.

They were wrong. All he said was "Thanks. You're very kind," and walked away, leaving the burger pods where they lay.

Another "opportunity for leadership" came with an idea designed to change the world, or at least change the small part in which I worked. This effort would address the reality that rural clinics that serve mentally ill people have a hard time recruiting psychiatrists. Most psychiatrists work in urban or suburban settings. The administrative leaders in my clinic worked constantly to recruit psychiatrists, with mixed success.

I had worked in this setting long enough to be aware that general medical providers add to their limited resources by making use of "physician extenders," specifically, Physician Assistants and Family Nurse Practitioners. These individuals receive a level of training sufficient to work in partnership with and under the supervision of a physician, performing basic services for common medical problems. Doctors are then freed up to address more complex patients. Why, it was asked, does psychiatry not have this kind of staff?

I embraced the idea but soon enough found that a significant number of doctors opposed the use of physician extenders or assistants. They saw it as an intrusion into the turf and authority of MDs. Permission for use of this resource was grudgingly given and tightly controlled by the state medical board, through a formal and complex application process. Furthermore, strict requirements for supervision by the sponsoring physician had to be followed and documented. Even more daunting was the fact that the use of physician extenders in psychiatry had never been approved by the medical board. I couldn't find out whether this was due to rejection of such applications or that no one had ever tried.

Seeing this as a potential change-the-world moment, and one that would actually do some good in my rural, underserved part of the world, I received permission from my workplace administrative leaders to make the effort. I did my homework; I talked to the general medical doctors in the area about how physician extenders worked in their practice. Those who employed them were universally positive and supportive of the concept and of my efforts to use them in the mental health world.

I approached the Board of Medical Examiners first with a notarized and lengthy letter of application followed by an in-person hearing in front of the members of the board in Raleigh. The setting resembled a courtroom, with nine white male doctors arrayed in front of me as I stood before them. A stenographer sat on one side of the "judges," the administrative director of the board on the other. The physician head of the board sat in the middle shuffling papers, making no eye contact at first. Looking up quickly, he began with, "So, tell us a little more about how this idea of yours would work."

It wasn't hard to read the cold skepticism on the faces of all of the doctors who faced me. I decided that my best foot forward was to make reference to the doctors with whom I had talked back in the community. "Well, I guess the first thing I would like to say is that it's an idea that fits within the community in which I practice. I've made a point to run this idea past the local docs and they think it makes sense."

Before I could add anything else, the chair of the group held up both hands, motioning for me to stop. He looked directly at me over his glasses on the end of his nose, hunched his shoulders and leaned forward, resting his weight on both hands. "Let's get one thing straight, Dr. Bridges. I am not a 'doc,' and I don't appreciate you referring to your colleagues in that way. We are physicians and I'll ask you to use that term of respect when you speak."

I was speechless. I thought my heart might stop because most of my blood was in my reddened face. Then I was angry. It occurred to me that the outcome of this meeting was a forgone conclusion. I considered arguing with him, but quickly decided on another approach, holding on to the hope I might still prevail.

"I understand your concern. I meant no disrespect...but...I apologize for the inappropriate informality."

He settled back into his chair without comment, and I interpreted this as permission to continue my presentation. When my ten-minute description of how this would bring services to a needy population was complete, I stood silent before them for a very long sixty seconds. The board leader looked first to the left, then to the right at the other members, "Any questions? Any comments?"

A single supporter spoke up, "Not sure I see any reason to turn this down."

The leader did not respond, but addressed me, "Thank you for coming. You'll get a letter from us within the month describing the conditions under which you may proceed."

As it turned out, the outcome of the meeting was pre-determined. The law clearly stipulated the physician extender provisions for what I was proposing. The letter I received was simple nuts and bolts about how I needed to interact with any "extender" under my supervision.

As far as I know, this was the first such approval for a psychiatric physician extender in NC. We subsequently hired a woman out of the University of North Carolina Family Nurse Practitioner program. She brought to our clinic general medical skills equal to my own and enthusiastically embraced new learning about treating psychiatric disorders.

Not all of the "great" ideas I came up with over the years worked out as well, but I did learn a valuable lesson. When one sets out to change things, there will always be people who see themselves as losing something: status, power, money, or something else.

Trying to Learn from Experience.
What is this Thing Called a Diagnosis?

A fundamental concept taught in medical school is about how to make a "diagnosis." To call something a "disease" one should have information on a number of factors. At a minimum, a disease must have a consistent presentation, including a set of physical findings or lab tests, along with reported perceptions, that is, subjective symptoms from the patient. It should also progress over time in a predictable way, and should respond to specific interventions, or treatments, in an expected pattern.

One of the advantages of practicing in the same community for a long time is that one has the opportunity to see people over time. Without this continuity with the patient, the clinician is often left with a "snapshot in time" that lacks full criteria to give the illness a definitive name. In the rural mental health facility in which I worked for three decades, I had not only my own longevity, but old records from a time before my involvement with certain patients.

I first encountered a man in his early twenties who presented with severe symptoms of anxiety including panic attacks. He had also been binge-drinking, but it was not hard to sort out that he was self-medicating his anxiety with alcohol. A standard non-addicting medication for anxiety promptly alleviated his symptoms and he returned to a successful and productive life.

In this situation I had the good fortune of reviewing his records from an old chart when he was eight years old. The primary diagnosis then was "school phobia" with further descriptions of oppositional and defiant behaviors. "School phobia" is now considered to be a type of anxiety disorder but at that time was not understood in that way. Some thought it to imply fundamental disruptions, if not abuse and neglect, within the family structure.

I worked at that clinic long enough that I saw him a third time, fifteen years later. This time he presented with a very different set of symptoms. He complained of profound and enduring feelings of depression, but no anxiety, no substance use. He remained functional and productive in his blue-collar job. He came in only due to the urging of his family who noticed his sadness, and because of his good experiences at the clinic earlier in his life. This time, his depression responded to a medication very similar to the one that alleviated his anxiety a decade and a half ago.

In psychiatry, there exists an argument about whether a patient can have significantly different diagnoses over time. For instance, could someone fit the criteria for schizophrenia at one point and at other times exhibit symptoms more consistent with bipolar disorder, or a serious and enduring depressive disorder? Alternatively, perhaps the person making the diagnosis simply is not doing a sufficiently thorough job of assessing and assigning diagnosis.

This man had been seen at the clinic three times with significantly different symptoms each time. My point? The thing that we call diagnosis can be a "fuzzy" thing.

Impostors, Puzzlements, and When Nothing is Clear

During my medical school years, a time when I had already made up my mind that I was choosing psychiatry as a specialty, a controversial study was published in *Science* magazine. The 1973 article, called "Being Sane in Insane Places," focused on the lack of clarity in the diagnostic process of psychiatry. Indeed, the author of the study proposed that psychiatrists could not tell the difference between those who were mentally ill and those who were not.

To prove the thesis of the study, the researcher recruited a number of "normal" subjects and coached them in a strategy whereby they gained admission to a psychiatric ward. The subjects were instructed to act normally after admission and state that the symptoms reported on admission had resolved. Despite the resolution of their presenting pathology, the subjects were given major diagnoses and prescribed powerful psychiatric medications.

Although the article in *Science* was generally discredited as poorly designed and some of the data actually "faked," the study at the time gained wide acclaim in the general public. More importantly, key leaders in psychiatry, despite their disdain for the study in question, agreed that the diagnostic process and criteria for specific disorders needed revision. This led over the next decade to a major revision of the diagnostic nomenclature and underlying criteria. The change is best described as moving from a theory-based model to a descriptive approach.

When I first read the article, I was sympathetic to the basic premise, that the issue of what "crazy" really means is worthy of debate. More specifically, throughout my training and extending into the years I was in practice, I was reminded regularly that I and my profession should approach our deliberations and proclamations with humility. One of the most striking lessons came in my first year of training. This involved a patient I will give the pseudonym of "Timmy." I choose that name because of the childlike way in which he first presented.

Timmy presented for admission at Dorothea Dix Hospital, the state psychiatric hospital, one of the two inpatient training sites for me and my fellow psychiatric residents. A tall, athletic, and strikingly handsome 20 something man, Timmy stated that he had become suicidal due to having involved himself in destructive relationships. In a meek, pleading, and vulnerable voice, he added that this was the pattern of his life, abused and neglected since childhood. He pointed out several faded scars on his face as testament to his mistreatment.

He wanted to be admitted in order to start his life over again. I and the staff who helped admit him felt immediately protective of him.

Several hours into his admission to the ward he experienced a fainting episode and was prevented from falling by the quick action of a nurse standing nearby. As she lowered him to the floor, he grabbed her breasts, one in each hand and held on tightly as he wiggled and quivered in what appeared to be some version of a seizure. The nurse was not injured but shaken emotionally. Nevertheless, she and the rest of us gave him the benefit of the doubt regarding the legitimacy of his seizure, as we settled him into a bed and called for a medical staff consultation beyond what was usually done for routine admissions.

The consultation, complete with electroencephalogram and electrocardiogram, found no treatable cause of his fainting event. For the next several days, in discussions with the staff, our empathy for him and his troubled life began to fade. A visitor to one of the other patients reported that he had offered money if the visitor would bring him alcohol. Our empathy disappeared when we learned he had promised money to a social work student if she would go with him to his room and let him touch her under her clothes.

A senior psychiatrist on the ward interviewed him and pronounced judgement. "These 'predatory sociopaths' do show up on the ward from time to time. Fortunately, they are rare enough that you may never see another one, at least while you're here. They should be hospitalized and studied, but not here. We probably should call the police and have him arrested, but the whole thing would probably turn into a he-said-she-said thing. So, let's just discharge him and have security walk him off the campus. Make sure you write all this up, in detail, and put a separate note in the file in admissions."

A month later I rotated on a ward in Chapel Hill's NC Memorial Hospital, the other inpatient training site for residents. Ten or so of us student psychiatrists gathered for an early Monday morning conference. These conferences often covered patients and situations from the weekend work. One of my fellow resident psychiatrists presented a patient.

"I really need some help with this one," she began. The medical ward wants us to take this guy back, after he had a cardiac arrest on Saturday."

"After a cardiac arrest?" The senior psychiatrist appeared puzzled. "Was he on one of our wards when he had the arrest?"

"We had just walked onto the ward after I admitted him from the ER. I actually walked up with him to the ward. Right inside the door he fell flat on his face, really hard. I could tell he wasn't breathing and he had this gurgling sound with saliva pouring out of his mouth. So, I called a code on him. By the time the code team got there we got a pulse...but still not breathing on his own. We had managed to get enough air in him so he wasn't blue anymore. They tubed him and sent him to ICU."

"So, what is the medical service saying now?" the senior psychiatrist asked.

"They don't think he had an arrest. Nothing on EKG, no enzymes or anything else in the labs to show anything. They think he's faking." Puzzled looks filled the room.

A little light went on in my head. I asked, "Is this guy's name Timmy?"

"No, It's Willie..."

I interrupted her as she was again raising her opposition to taking him back to the psychiatric ward, "Is he a really handsome guy, about six-feet tall, athletic and with a few scars on his face?"

My colleague grew silent, and I asked one more question, "And does he talk in a little meek, childlike way."

"So how do you know this...this patient...what?"

I gave a quick summary of my experience with Timmy-at-Dix. Everyone in the room agreed I should visit this patient that may or may not be Timmy, this patient that may have been able to fake a cardiac arrest, tolerate having a tube placed in his trachea, plus all the needle sticks that go with treatment of a cardiac arrest.

The entire group walked the ten-minute trip through the hospital to the medical ward where the patient awaited a decision about the appropriate medical service to care for him. I, my resident colleague, and the senior psychiatrist entered the room while the others waited in the hall.

"Hi, Timmy," I said softly.

"Hey, doc!" he spoke enthusiastically. "Long time, no see."

"I hear you're going by Wille now?"

"You got it doc. Let me ask you a question. How many hospitals do you work at? Looks like I need to expand my territory."

A very different kind of puzzlement came years later when I was working in a rural mental health center. The receptionist buzzed my phone to say she had a strange situation in the outpatient waiting room. A woman had approached the front desk and announced she had an appointment with me at the present hour. The receptionist replied that the appointment time was already scheduled with someone else. While the person on the schedule had not yet arrived, the staff member explained she couldn't give away the appointment to someone else.

On the phone I asked for the name of the woman there at the desk asking to be seen.

"She says her name is Ruby, and says you'll know who she is. I don't have a last name so I can't look for a chart on her. I don't think I've ever seen her before."

"I don't think I have anyone named Ruby on my caseload, but I'll come out and speak to her." As I saw her across the waiting room, I did not recognize her. But she walked toward me and greeted me enthusiastically.

"Hi, Dr. Bridges, I'm on time for once."

As I looked closely at her face, she seemed familiar, but I still did not realize with whom I was talking. Walking past me and turning toward my office around the corner, she obviously knew the location of my room. I followed her and watched her make herself comfortable in one of the chairs used by patients. She remained silent and simply looked at me with a look of anticipation. By this time, I was starting to understand.

She finally spoke, "So have you figured it out yet?"

"Maybe, but I would prefer you tell me. I had someone on my schedule named Louise."

"Louise is a loser. She always gets here late. I know that pisses you off, but you never call her on it. Today you got Ruby, and today we're going to get somewhere."

I had never seen a patient with multiple personality disorder, or dissociative identity disorder (DID), the modern name for the condition. During my training, this was a diagnosis that was often discussed, but rarely encountered. A small but vocal group of current psychiatrists put forth the opinion that it is seldom seen because no one looks for it, no one asked the questions that would reveal the disorder. An equally vocal subset of the profession doubted the existence of DID. I was pretty sure at this moment that this was what I was seeing.

"So, what are we going to accomplish today?" I asked, following her lead.

"I'm going to tell you some things about old Louise. You don't know shit about her. I don't even know why the hell she comes here. I guess because someone told her to and she always does what people tell her to do. She's like that to most people, pitiful."

"What else can you tell me about Louise?"

"She's not always such a wimp. But you never get to see that. She's sneaky, and she's mean, and she's strong. You wouldn't believe some of the things she's capable of."

"Is that when she is Ruby?"

When I asked this question, she looked startled, and for just a moment I realized I had made a big mistake. I knew that, early on, the proper mode of questioning of someone with DID should be open ended and accepting, but I realized my question was confrontational.

But she was ready for me and pressed on. "No, not Ruby, you're not going to pin that one me. That would be Suzie. Suzie the dancer, the partier, the one that can just go off any place, any time, for nothing, for little bitty things. And what a mess she always makes." She pointed to a small scar on her chin. "This scar, that's Suzie's, not mine."

She paused, opened her purse and took out a cigarette, then remembered the clinic was non-smoking and snapped her purse back shut. She looked at me obviously waiting for another question. I took a moment to reflect on how "Ruby" could be so different in appearance from the woman I knew as Louise. Not only did she dress differently—best described as colorful and even provocative—but her whole manner of carrying herself and her facial expression were that of another person.

"So, you, Ruby, would never do the things that Suzie does." I asked cautiously.

"My job is to clean up the messes. It's a tough job."

I knew that Louise, or Ruby, or Suzie, came from a violent family, so I wasn't sure it was timely for me to know what kinds of messes she cleaned up—not just yet. But she moved on to another topic, one that I wanted to discuss. For the greater part of the hour, she laid out her motivation for coming today as Ruby. Simply put, she needed me to know that Louise was not the passive, helpless victim. Ruby went on to describe some modest, but important accomplishments within her family, mostly protecting others from harm by a man in the family.

She opened her purse again and took out the cigarette, "Do you mind if I just suck on this as long as I don't light it? I get all worked up sometimes when I talk about what Louise has to go through and the kinds of things I end up having to clean up."

In 40 years of psychiatric practice, I am aware of seeing three patients with DID. The patient named Louise, Ruby, Suzie, and a few other names, was the only one I saw for any length of time, over a decade. I saw Suzie only once and she revealed nothing of substance. The meeting was informative only in what she looked like. I had to do a little work with those staff who worked at the front desk to explain that Louise may come "disguised" at times, but if there was any question about who arrived at 3PM on Fridays, let me know and I would handle it.

Another situation that speaks to who is, and who is not, crazy happened before I even got to medical school. As a college undergraduate, I had a friend who told me the story of running afoul of her father when she was eighteen. She had the audacity to refuse to go to college after graduating from high school with top grades. Instead, she moved in with her boyfriend and got a job in a restaurant.

Her father was a man of some prominence in the small town where they lived, and he convinced the family doctor that her behavior showed clear evidence of mental illness. This took place in the late 1960s, a time when the signature of one physician, psychiatrist or otherwise, would get you committed to the state hospital for 30 days. No legal review, no court process; you were in for a month, if a doctor signed you in.

Once admitted, however, the staff at the mental hospital recognized immediately that she had no psychiatric disorder. Unable to do anything to shorten her stay, the staff made her an offer. They suggested that the time would go more quickly if she made herself useful. So, for the duration of her hospitalization, she became a "junior staff member" assisting the nurses who take care of some seriously mentally ill women. She gave patients baths, changed beds, and generally kept company and gave support to those who needed help.

Those of us hearing her story were outraged and some questioned what she would do to get back at her father. But she just shrugged and said, "No. Actually, it was one of the most interesting months of my life. I wouldn't have missed it for the world."

Shorts: Brief Interactions Short of a Full Story

But I'm Really Rich

One of my first experiences with finding out that things are not always what they seem came when I was in training at Dorothea Dix Hospital. A man was admitted over the weekend with what was clearly a psychotic disorder. He was quite incensed that we did not believe he was God, and he blamed others for the brawl he reportedly initiated at a movie theater. He did not sleep or eat for two days, but with medication he slowly calmed down and organized his thinking.

Yet he never gave up on his claim that he was very wealthy, and I finally agreed to call a phone number in Washington, DC and report his hospitalization to a specific person. The woman on the phone was very grateful for my call saying his family had been worried sick about him. The next day two black stretch limousines pulled up in front of the hospital. Two attorneys, with a court order from a local judge for his release, explained to me that some version of his latest hospitalization occurred every year or so. They thanked me enthusiastically.

Easy Money

I once treated a young man who had suffered a psychosis. He did well and for the duration of the time I followed him, he returned to his successful life. I included his family in many of the sessions, educating his parents about what the future might hold for their son. His father, clearly an intelligent man but not a health care professional, asked questions that suggested he had at least done some reading about his son's condition.

As we completed one session and stood at the door saying goodbye, I commented on the fact that the father asked very intelligent questions and asked him, "So have you read up on the kind of thing your son is going through?"

"Oh, I read about psychology all the time," he replied with a smile and added, "I always wanted to be a psychiatrist."

"Really?" I said with a smile on my face, thinking his statement might lead to further dialogue.

"Yeah, I always wanted to get my hands on that easy money."

Then he turned and walked away, not waiting for my reaction or comment.

Sweetest Fellow in the World

I greeted a new patient, accompanied by his mother and brother, in the mental health clinic. Mother spoke first, "Jackie's finally out of prison and we are all so happy he's back home. He's my sweet boy, just the best person I know. He'd give you the shirt off his back and button it up for you. It was so unfair he was locked up all those years."

I smiled, nodded my response to her words and accepted a vigorous handshake from Jackie and then from his brother. After thanking mother and brother for coming, I invited Jackie into my office for the initial interview.

After going through the usual process of finding out why he needed to come to the mental health clinic, and the necessary background information, we inevitably addressed the question of his prison stay. He seemed open and forthcoming with the information that he spent nine years in prison for murder.

I asked gently leading questions about how it had all happened, and he summed it up for me. "I never meant to kill anybody, but when you're hittin' a nigger with a tire tool, you're just not sure how hard you're hittin' him 'til he stops movin'. Anyhows, it was his wife that dragged me into the bed, not the other way around. The man shouldn't jumped me."

I'm not sure if my face betrayed a reaction of any sort. I was far enough along in my life and my career to have become aware of all manner of the human experience, including the violence, so what Jackie said did not shock or surprise me. I believe I was able to stay focused on my task, to help this man who was my patient.

Nantucket

Working at an alcohol and drug abuse diagnosis and treatment center, I helped admit a young man to our admissions and observation area. In this unit, known as MSO, the patients could stay under medically supervised observation for up to 24 hours to see what kind of further treatment is needed. This patient mumbled, slurred, and stammered out a need for detoxification from a variety of drugs, primarily alcohol. Clearly anxious, he had a marked startle response to any noise behind him.

His general appearance was striking. Well over six feet tall, he had shoulder length blond hair, multiple metal piercings in his ears and nose, and he was dressed in a t-shirt that sported a confederate flag on the front. Over the t-shirt he wore a leather jacket with an American flag on the back. The American flag also had a large peace symbol decal overlaying the stripes, and he wore ornately decorated cowboy boots.

We got to work. After about four hours, the medication that we gave him both calmed him and made him more alert. We helped him with a sponge bath that greatly improved his body aroma. After he eagerly confessed his descent into depravity and pledged himself to a new path in life, he drifted into a nap.

Thirty minutes later, as I sat in the nurses' station writing up his evaluation, he came running out of the room. He held his pants, shirt, and jacket in one hand and his boots in the other as he spoke. "Hey, man...I just figured something out. Nantucket is playing in Wilmington tonight...I ain't missin' Nantucket for this shit. It's my favorite band!"

We watched through the large glass double side doors as he ran to his car. No one even thought about trying to retrieve the hospital gown.

Trip to the Moon

Many of the professors who taught me were part "showmen" and entertainer. Their stage was the diagnostic conference room and their performance consisted of interviewing patients in front of other clinicians. In the best situation, this served the benefit of the patient and the various students. One popular psychiatrist, who conducted interviews on an inpatient ward, characteristically refused any background history before he performed the interview. He took pride in the fact that from an interview alone he could reconstruct the patient's history, uncover key early developmental influences, and make an accurate diagnosis, all in about an hour. He was usually right, and his conferences were well attended. When he was wrong, it was usually a matter of nuance or degree.

One patient completely baffled him. The patient denied experiencing any emotional symptoms or life stresses, and stated his only concern was the need to get out of the hospital and back to his life. He described loving parents, good relationships with several siblings, and a marriage free of conflict. He had no idea how or why he ended up on the ward, and all in attendance clearly saw him as intelligent, calm and composed. One could feel a bit of tension in the room as the customary time allotted for the interview approached an end. The professor uncharacteristically showed just a hint of frustration on his face.

At that point, the patient yawned, and the professor posed a simple question.

"You look a little tired. Did you sleep well last night?"

The patient suddenly pushed his chair back, stood up and screamed, "Hell no I didn't sleep! You couldn't either if you had to pack your suitcase for a trip to the moon! Are you gonna let me out of here or what?" The needed information was thus obtained.

Women in Medicine

In the 1970s, most medical students were men. Only about 10% of my class was female. I recall one incident that illustrated not only this numerical imbalance but the depth of feeling by some men doctors against women in medicine.

I remember this encounter, mainly from the punchline, between an older male doctor and a female medical student, but the fundamental nature of the interaction is clear even after many years. It most likely took place in the large lecture hall, or could have been in one of many smaller gatherings of learners.

During the lecture by this older male physician, the issue of the lack of women doctors came up. One of my female classmates had asked a question that included her wondering if having some women on the staff of one particular clinical program might be advantageous to the patients.

After a short pause, the man replied with a question, sarcasm undisguised. "So what specialty are you going into, little lady?"

She replied in a matter-of-fact way, "Probably a general practice...or internal medicine."

"Well..." he continued with a visible and audible sigh, "I guess if you want to spend your time massaging prostates, that's your choice...but I'm not sure you're cut out for it."

In 2010 I attended my nephew's medical school graduation ceremony in Boston. A majority of the class were women, and most of them appeared to be of Indian-Asian-Pacific Islander descent. I remember thinking that if I lived long enough, all of my doctors would be women.

Municipal Bonds

During my first year of psychiatric training, my attention was often drawn to a charismatic, well-liked third year resident. I watched him evolve over the course of the year. His shoulder length hair turned into a neat traditional short cut. Bell bottomed jeans became creased slacks and just as often, a suit and necktie. A pregnant wife and the need to have a job beyond the training world probably had something to do with his sartorial metamorphosis.

Shortly before his graduation I came face to face with him as he hurried down a hospital hallway. He stopped and positioned himself directly in front of me and spoke with a serious demeanor.

"Drew. Two words. Municipal Bonds."

Still two years before I would need to face the demands of his situation, I replied. "But what happened to cosmic consciousness?"

A genuine—or at least well-acted—expression of bewilderment fell across his face. After a short pause, he spoke. "But Drew, they are tax free!"

Then he turned quickly and walked away.

Friends Are Where You Find Them

For over two decades, I treated a developmentally delayed woman, said to have an IQ about fifty-five, plus other learning difficulties. My main role was to prescribe a very modest dose of medication for mild to moderate depression. I also counseled her parents about the larger issues of how she lived in the world.

This woman was extremely fortunate that she had very capable and financially comfortable parents. She was less fortunate in that her parents considered her incapable of surviving outside the immediate family. In many ways they treated her as a child. Her parents still bought her baby dolls for Christmas. The only social contact other than her parents, and an older brother, was church attendance. I believed that some of her depression was loneliness and boredom, and I made regular attempts to have them enlist her in some of the local supportive programs for people with intellectual disabilities. These local programs were quite strong, and regularly honored by state officials as innovative leaders in such efforts.

The parents always resisted, describing her as helpless and vulnerable. In only one instance did I convince the father to visit one of the programs to see for himself what they were like. He returned and reported, "I'm sure these programs are good for some people, but not for her." He then cupped his hand around one side of his face, leaned in close to me and whispered, "And they have

Black people there. If one of them tried to take advantage of her, she'd have no way to defend herself. She'd be helpless." I gave up, for the moment.

I followed this patient until both her parents had passed away. She was in her early forties when they died. Working with her older brother, we assisted her with admission to a small group home, which came with membership in a day program that provided her with social and educational experiences.

On one of her subsequent appointments with me in the clinic, I went out to greet her in the waiting room. From down the hall I could see her on a couch beside a staff member at the group home who had brought her to the appointment. He was a dark-skinned Black man, well over six feet tall, and by my estimate weighed close to three hundred pounds.

I paused for just a moment to take in the sight that would have panicked her father. As I slowly approached them, I watched as they carried on in an animated conversation. She reached over and slapped him on the knee, both laughing enthusiastically. I am quite sure this was the first time I ever saw her laugh.

I followed her for at least five more years, until I left the clinic. Staff reports included the description that she "was more like a staff member than a resident" at the group home, and she had a terrific sense of humor. One staff member said, "I'm not really sure she's actually mentally retarded, but that's just my opinion."

What is Real?

Early in my career I treated a man who had been removed from his position in one of the U.S Government's national security agencies. While he apparently performed his duties well for over two decades, his superiors judged that he had become mentally unstable and unreliable, reporting facts that no one could confirm, some bizarre and impossible. He fought his discharge from employment, explaining his situation in terms of various conspiracies against him both foreign and local.

The agency treated him respectfully and with kindness, as far as I could tell. My interaction with his superiors was limited to one phone call that was informative in both the process and content of his difficulties. He had been in several mental hospitals and at one point required a legal constraining order to limit his contact with his previous employer. Neither I nor the others who treated him psychiatrically doubted that he had a mental disorder.

At one point I took a phone call from my patient. I don't recall the topic of the call. In the middle of our conversation the phone line made a strange beep then went dead. I quickly reconnected and apologized for the interruption.

"Sorry for that," I said. "I'm not sure what happened to the phone."

"That's okay, I haven't had the use of a phone that wasn't tapped in a long time."

I remember thinking how unfortunate that this phone bleep happened when it did. It clearly played into his illness and made my job more difficult. I later shared this incident with a more experienced psychiatrist.

My colleague replied, "Why do you think he wasn't right? You think that agency wouldn't be keeping tabs on what he was doing?"

What is that bit of wisdom? Just because you are paranoid does not mean that someone is not watching you.

Traditional Forms of Healing

Practicing in a rural area will almost certainly acquaint you with traditional or alternative methods of healing. I greeted a woman in the waiting room who was accompanied by her husband. He always came with her to the appointment. As we walked down the hallway, I saw he was carrying a small tin can in one hand, filled with some aromatic liquid, his thumb immersed in the liquid. I asked him about it.

"It's kerosene. Got a bad cut on my thumb. Nothin' better than kerosene."

This triggered an old memory of my father and my grandmother using kerosene to disinfect scratches and cuts, but that was a long time ago.

"Can I take a look at it? I actually have a lot of experience with cuts."

During my last year in medical school, I served a two-month rotation in a rural hospital emergency room. The doctors who covered emergencies were understandably bored with some simple tasks, so they gave me a tutorial and called me for simple cuts. I sewed up at least fifty simple lacerations in those two months. Most were hands and feet but also some on faces. This was 1973 and farm communities did not get plastic surgeons to keep them looking pretty.

Once my patient agreed to let me look at his cut, I lifted the man's thumb out of the kerosene. I did not actually see bone, but it was bad. I got the director of the clinic, who was a nurse, to assist me in getting out the first aid kit and we cleaned and bandaged the wound with copious amounts of topical antiseptics. It had laid open too long to suture it. It would heal ugly, but I was pretty sure it would heal, no sign of infection and he did not have a fever. I urged him to go to a family doctor or an emergency room for follow up.

He just smiled at me. We gave him all the gauze, topical antiseptics, and bandages we had.

I encountered another "cultural" remedy in the form of a quart jar filled with a variety of plant roots. I recognized carrots and turnips, but many others I could not name. My patient explained that the local root doctor had soaked the roots in olive oil for a month and they were now ready to consume, starting with drinking the olive oil. She had been told to drink a full cup of it every day until it was gone, then eat all the roots, one each day until they were finished. This should help her depression, according to the root doctor.

She asked my advice about the wisdom of consuming this "medicine." I essentially punted, saying there was no way I could advise her, but I was pretty sure the olive oil would have a cleansing effect on her gastrointestinal tract. She left it with me and I kept it for a while. The contents ultimately grew some very colorful molds near the top of the jar.

Adventures with Lawyers

Another "benefit" of being seen as having experience, if not wisdom, is the request from lawyers to assist in defense of their clients. Not being an expert in forensic issues, I almost always declined such opportunities. However, one request caught my attention.

The attorney's client was a physician who had been called before the North Carolina State Board of Medical Examiners for an ethics complaint having to do with questionable medication prescribing practices. The attorney requested I help him prepare a defense based on the fact that the doctor practiced in a rural, underserved area, and should be held to a different "community standard" compared to other doctors who practiced in resource rich settings.

I agreed to review the available documentation about the complaint. What I found was a physician who gave out stunningly generous amounts of addictive medications. Almost as egregious, he had an aversion to record keeping. Patient chart notes seldom showed any attempt at a specific diagnosis, other than pain and nervousness, and no chart record of prescriptions written matched with what the patients took to the local pharmacy. It was a local pharmacist who had reported him to the medical board.

At the appointed time, I got a call from the lawyer, "So, Dr. Bridges, do you think a defense based on community standard will work?"

I replied slowly. "Here is what your client needs to do. He needs to go before the board, fall down on his knees, clasp his hands in prayer position, and beg for forgiveness and request an opportunity for re-education about appropriate prescribing practices, the necessity of record keeping, and the value of making a specific diagnosis."

"Really?" The attorney did not try to conceal his surprise in his one-word reply. He sputtered out a few more words that seemed a bit defiant and even angry.

"Yes really." I calmly gave him a brief review of what I thought would happen if he tried to fight the medical board. He seemed grateful by the time we finished our call. He paid me.

They Told Me I Couldn't Do It

Joe had spent most of his life in mental institutions. With an IQ of around 65, poorly controlled seizures from birth, and outbreaks of anger and violence, his family was unable to provide for him.

He had at some point been given a diagnosis of schizophrenia, but there was little documentation to justify it. Nevertheless, each return home, at all stages of his life, ended in conflict and chaos, so he lived in one institution or another throughout his life.

Then came the 1980s and significant funding for mental health programs to transition people like Joe into supportive housing and a "wrap-around" of services to enable him to succeed. At age 50 he was discharged from a state mental hospital to a supervised apartment living program. A team of mental health staff visited him multiple times each day. I prescribed his psychiatric medications and consulted with his neurologist about his seizures.

A life in institutions, however, could not get in the way of Joe's obsession with cars and motorcycles. He brought me form after form from the Division of Motor Vehicles for me to fill out so he could receive driver's education and get his license. But I had to be honest on the form, and my documentation of his poorly controlled seizures and sedating medication always led to a denial by the Department of Motor Vehicles.

Otherwise, Joe seemed to thrive outside the institutions. He spent peaceful weekends at his elderly mother's home and was accepted by her church and into the homes of her neighbors. He took pride in his own apartment. Under supervision of staff, he learned to cook simple meals.

Late one afternoon in the clinic I got a call from the front desk. The receptionist said Joe was outside in the parking lot and wanted to see me. Not fully understanding the request, I replied, "I don't see Joe on my schedule today."

"He's not looking for an appointment, he just wants to show you something in the parking lot."

Still puzzled by what was happening, never having treated a patient in the parking lot, I agreed to go outside. As I walked from my office to the waiting room, the receptionist added, "I think this is something you really want to see."

Just outside the front door, I came face to face with Joe, straddling a small, motorized bicycle, a football helmet held proudly under his arm. He also wore a smile that filled up the day, and told his story, his voice broken up by short bursts of giggles. His first words were, "They told me I couldn't do it. But I did. I did it. I got my bike!"

On the weekends home with his mother, Joe had done sufficient odd jobs and mowed enough lawns in his neighborhood to earn and save $200.00, just enough to buy the bike from a local shade-tree mechanic. He had cleared it with the local police that he needed no license for the bike. I expressed my surprise and my genuine admiration for his accomplishment and watched him ride away, the small motor popping like a sputtering kitchen mixer.

I did not express my fear for him, other than telling him to be careful, and indeed the bike did not last much more than a month. He crashed it into the side of a police car that was stopped at a red traffic light. He was not injured and ultimately agreed to be satisfied with the fact that he had done something that "they" never believed he could do.

Joe died several years later in an event related to his seizures. He could have lived longer in an institution. But I will never forget the day he pulled up to the clinic on his bike, glowing with pride. I have never seen a bigger smile or a happier man.

Best Show in Town

I heard from several of my patients that they spent time attending local court proceedings for their entertainment value.

"It's better than the soaps," one young man commented, "You wouldn't believe some of the things you see go on in that courthouse. But it don't really get good unless Judge Claude is the judge."

Then I happened to get a subpoena to testify as a medical expert in Judge Claude's court. Expert witnesses, even doctors, must be there when the session starts, and wait until their case comes up in order. As I sat waiting for my turn, I witnessed the judge in action on another case.

A middle-aged man stood before the judge for failure to meet child support payments. "But I got no job and no money, your honor. I got nothin.' I'm livin' on my momma's back porch and if she didn't feed me, I guess I'd starve. There just ain't no work out there for me." Head lowered, hands clasped behind his back, moving his weight from one foot to the other, the man appeared ready to cry. Judge Claude wiped his forehead, clearly considering his options.

A voice rang out from the back of the courtroom. "I can get that man a job!"

Judge Claude motioned for the man who called out to come to the bench. He took the man's name and asked what he did for a living and what kind of job he had in mind. Satisfied with the answers, Judge Claude rubbed his chin for about half a minute.

"Okay," the judge said, taking a deep breath, "I'm glad you can get this man a job. But what I'm really interested in is getting some money for his kids. I'll give him two weeks to pay the clerk at least two back payments on that child support. A decent paying job should take care of that. If I don't see that money, I'm locking you both up for thirty days. Dismissed."

Doctors and Toys

Early in my medical school years, I already was almost certainly going to choose psychiatry as my specialty, but I remember the day I made up my mind for good. It was the day a trauma surgeon walked into the large lecture hall to speak to my class of second year medical students.

"How are you going to decide what specialty to pursue?" A tall, handsome, physically fit man, he posed the question in a musing, reflective manner as he positioned a large cardboard box on a table in front of the lectern.

"Will it be about money?" He reached into the box to begin assembling a number of glass bottles and plastic tubes.

"What about lifestyle? Will you need to be home for dinner every night?" He then explained that the apparatus he displayed was a device to remove excess fluid when it accumulates in the space between the lung and the chest wall. He explained how to cut into the chest and how to position the device to relieve the excess fluid.

He then looked up at us and said, "No one going to take me up on my question about choosing a specialty? What about saving the world? Like being a hero? Looking for applause and respect?"

One student spoke, "I think I want to do something that actually gives me a relationship with patients, some intimacy, I guess."

The surgeon paused briefly, the hint of a frown on his face as he spoke. "Okay, does having your hands in the guts of a gunshot victim qualify as a form of intimacy?"

Without waiting for an answer from my classmate, the surgeon picked up the conversation. "Forget about all of that. Forget money, lifestyle, and that kind of thing. Ask yourself if there is a part of medicine that you think about and read about when you don't need to. Is there something you go to bed thinking about and wake up thinking about? That's what you choose."

He directed our attention back to his display of medical devices. "This is what I do. These are my toys. I can't believe that I get paid for using this stuff and that it actually does good things for people. Find something that hooks you like this did me. And just hope that if you ever need emergency surgery that the surgeon isn't pissed off because he's missing dinner or a movie."

I looked down at the small pile of books on the floor beside me. Among the medical books was a copy of *Nausea* by Sartre. This literary illustration of what some call examples of mental illness was not assigned reading. It was the kind of thing I chose to read, even with a busy medical school curriculum. Decision confirmed.

Viking Physician

During a vacation in the United Kingdom, one of my favorite places was the city of York, where a fully intact Viking ship had been discovered during an excavation for the foundation of a new building. Tourists were allowed to stand on an elevated viewing platform and treated to an informative description of the ship undergoing preservation efforts. Of course, we were invited to purchase various merchandise celebrating the find. I chose a bright yellow t-shirt emblazoned across the front in red and black with the face of a fierce Viking warrior.

On the flight back home, I settled into my airplane seat, wearing my impressive purchase. Since I wore my hair shoulder length at the time, and sported a full beard, I was sure I struck fear into the hearts of my fellow passengers. The takeoff was uneventful, and I looked out the window to see the land below give way to the vast ocean.

Preparing to open a small airline bottle of rum to add to my Coca-Cola, a message came over the intercom, "Is there a physician onboard? We have a passenger who needs attention." I waited a full minute, hoping a surgeon or at least a non-psychiatrist would step forward. No luck. I raised my hand to volunteer my services.

I followed the attendant to the back of the plane and introduced myself to an older woman in obvious respiratory difficulty. She looked up at the long-haired bearded man come to help her. I saw confusion on her face. When she looked a bit lower and saw the image of the Viking, I saw terror. I smiled, hoping that would calm her. The attendant spoke reassuringly to her. The woman's daughter stepped in to give me more information.

Fortunately for all of us, I knew commercial airliners were pressurized at less than sea level strength. This woman had recently had a lung removed due to cancer. She was going to the United States essentially to say goodbye to family members. In this airplane, she was breathing air equivalent to that of Denver, the "mile-high city." She needed oxygen, and fortunately the plane had that.

Despite the relatively simple diagnosis and treatment, I was ushered into the cockpit to sit in a fold-down chair behind the pilots and talk on the radio with an airline physician, just to be sure that I did the right thing. I doubt I would get in the cockpit today, post 9-11. We agreed all was in order, especially when the woman breathed more easily with the help from the oxygen tank.

Returning to my seat, I screwed the cap tightly back on the little bottle of rum and put it aside. I'm very sensitive to alcohol, in other words, a cheap drunk. I get bloodshot eyes easily from just a small amount of liquor and I'm told that I show a dumb look on my face. It was bad enough that this woman had to endure a long haired, bearded, Viking doctor. If it had been a long haired, bearded, bloodshot eyed, drunk Viking doctor it might just have killed her.

Nevertheless, by rendering aid on the flight, I thought I might get a free ticket somewhere. Three weeks later I received a thank-you letter from the airline.

Watch Your Language

At one point in my work in a rural community mental health center, I organized educational placements for student psychiatrists in their second year of training. One of the educational objectives was to introduce them to fundamental concepts of psychotherapy. Patients were carefully selected for them as appropriate to their level of training. I had the privilege of supervising one of the students, a very talented young doctor.

He presented to me one case of a woman who was clearly mistreated by an insensitive and at least verbally abusive husband. She had told him she was going to stand up to him, to confront him about his "meanness" to her.

Worried about her safety, the student cautioned her to "choose your shots" carefully. She responded with a chuckle, "yeah, I'll just fire a few warning shots over his head."

A few weeks later my supervisee came to me somewhat shaken. His patient had indeed fired some warning shots, and further reported, "I think I got his attention, but it messed up the wall and one window pretty bad."

It had taken him a few moments to realize she was speaking literally and that she had discharged most of the bullets of a handgun "safely" over his head in their bedroom.

The young doctor and I had an interesting discussion about the power of words.

What's in a Name?

My last short story is one of my favorite from the many case conferences I attended. The more senior members of the gathering spoke in depth and at length about the name given to the patient by his parents. His short lifetime of trouble, they opined, was due to a gender-neutral name. It was said that he was unable to form a core identity and know how to relate to others because of confusion about masculine and feminine issues.

I looked around the conference table and took note of the fact that two of the professionals attending the meeting were women named Ronnie. Two men in the room were named Rene and Drew, respectively. I left the meeting with a smile on my face and thinking about the county song named "A Boy Named Sue" by Johnny Cash.

Afterword

There are many more stories I could have told, but I held back, for various reasons. In some stories, it would have been difficult to protect the identities of the patients. I directly treated or otherwise interacted with a few people who were at least regionally well-known public figures. How I wish I could tell those stories. Severe mental illness and disorders of character and impulse are present in all sociocultural classes and professions. Some hide this better than others; money helps. All professions seem to have about the same ratio of saints to sinners. Sometimes doctors, lawyers, and preachers seem to be overrepresented in the sinners' category.

I also wanted to make me, and my own flaws and sometimes cluelessness, drive the action. I hope I have given an interested reader a useful and perhaps unique look at what goes on in the world of doctors and psychiatrists particularly. I did not confess all. It would be just too embarrassing.

In finishing this book, I am reminded of one professor who at the time I knew him I did not fully appreciate. He often interrupted students who presented cases to him with some approximation of these words: "You are giving me dry and not very interesting facts about this patient. I don't know what to do with what you are telling me, because it really tells me nothing about this patient's life. He has a story and I want you to tell me his story." I have tried to tell you stories that reveal more than any clinical report or psychological test.

This book is also my story, or a part of it. I am more than my work, and unlike some who can't seem to leave a profession behind, I retired joyfully. Now if I could just stop writing.

Printed in the United States
by Baker & Taylor Publisher Services